A CHRISTIAN PERSPECTIVE ON

TWENTY-FIRST CENTURY SPIRITUALITY

BRUCE G. FREDERICKSON

SAINT LOUIS

Edited by Ed Grube and Rodney Rathmann

This publication is available in braille and in large print for the visually impaired. Write to the Library for the Blind, 1333 S. Kirkwood Rd., St. Louis, MO 63122-7295; or call 1-800-433-3954.

1 2 3 4 5 6 7 8 9 10   08 07 06 05 04 03 02 01 00 99

CONTENTS

PREFACE

ABOUT THE CHRISTIAN PERSPECTIVE SERIES

Hasn't each of us often been confronted with an issue that challenges us? It nags at our patience, frustrating us in our desire to honor God in the way we handle, manage, and react to the issue in our daily life. We struggle, unable to find the right approach or perspective. Some issues may even cause us to question God and His power and presence in our life. At times we may feel helpless and weak in the way we react to an issue—we become baby Christians wondering if we will ever grow up. Feeling unworthy and ill-equipped to be the witnesses of Jesus in an unreceptive and apathetic world, we may echo the sentiments of Agur of old, who marveled at the greatness of God in comparison to his own inadequacies. He said,

> I am the most ignorant of men; I do not have a man's understanding. I have not learned wisdom, nor have I knowledge of the Holy One. Who has gone up to heaven and come down? Who has gathered up the wind in the hollow of His hands? Who has wrapped up the waters in His cloak? Who has established all the ends of the earth? What is His name, and the name of His Son? Tell me if you know! (Proverbs 30:2–4)

Fortunately, God didn't leave us alone to struggle with those things that challenge us and cause us to pause when we don't know what to think or how to respond. With a love for us that reaches back before the beginning of time and connects us with a crude wooden cross that stood in Palestine some 2000 years ago, God cares about our everyday concerns. He has given us the direction, counsel, and power of His holy Word to help us live life in joyful response to all that He has done for us through Jesus, His Son and our Savior.

Each title in the *Christian Perspective* series has been designed to provide the insights and reflections of an author who has personally confronted an issue that touches us and challenges our life of faith in one way or another. The author has sought to apply the counsel of God's holy Word to this topic and has put his or her thoughts and conclusions in writing to give others confronted with the same issue a "jump start" in their thinking.

The *Christian Perspective* series has been designed in the book-study format, organized in chapters and suitable for either individual use or group study. Following the reading of each chapter, questions have been provided to further stimulate your thinking and to serve as discussion starters if the book study is being used in a small-group setting. May God bless you as you explore the topic of this course.

SUGGESTIONS FOR USING THIS COURSE IN A GROUP SETTING

Select a leader for the course or a leader for the day. It will be the leader's responsibility to keep the discussion moving and to help involve everyone.

Emphasize sharing. Your class will work best if the participants feel comfortable with one another and if all feel that their contributions to the class discussion are important and useful. Take the necessary time at the beginning of the course to get to know one another. You might share names, occupations, hobbies, and so on. Share what you expect to gain from this course. Take some time at the beginning of each class session to allow participants to share experiences and news items from the week that relate to your study. Be open and accepting. Don't force anyone to speak. The course will be most helpful if participants willingly share deep feelings, problems, doubts, fears, and joys. That will require building an atmosphere of openness, trust, and caring about one another. Take time to build relationships among participants. That time will not be wasted!

Find ways to keep the session informal. Meet in casual surroundings. Arrange seating so participants can face one another. Ask volunteers to provide refreshments.

Depend on the Holy Spirit. Expect His presence. He will guide you and cause you to grow through the study of His holy Word. He has promised that His Word will not return empty (Isaiah 55:11).

But do not expect the Spirit to do your work for you!

Start early! Prepare well! As time permits, do additional reading about the topic.

Begin and end on time. Punctuality is a courtesy to everyone and can be a factor that will encourage discussion.

Keep the class moving. The leader should move the class along from section to section in the Study Guide. Limit your discussion to questions of interest to the participants. Be selective. You don't need to cover every question and every Bible verse.

Work to build up one another through your fellowship and study. You have your needs; other group members have theirs. Together you have a lot to gain.

Be sensitive to any participants who may have needs related to the specific topics discussed in this course.

Be a "gatekeeper." That means you may need to shut the gate of conversation on one person while you open it for someone else. Endeavor to involve everyone, especially those who hesitate to speak.

Expect and rejoice in God's presence and blessing as He builds your faith and enriches your life.

INTRODUCTION

Attitudes concerning the twenty-first century have been mixed. Some people have anticipated the twenty-first century with enthusiasm, others with fear. Questions surrounding the advent of the twenty-first century have reflected these attitudes.

- Will Judgment Day occur on the first day of the new millennium?
- Will we finally find a cure for dreaded diseases such as cancer, AIDS, and so on?
- Will all computers quit functioning because they are unable to adjust to the date 2000?
- Will society be thrown into turmoil because of the malfunction of millions of computers?
- Will the new millennium give people and nations another chance to demonstrate love and compassion to others?
- How will the world be different during the twenty-first century?

These questions and others have prompted much speculation. Although we may face many changes and challenges as we move into the years 2000, 2001, 2002, ..., one thing will remain constant:

> Because God wanted to make the unchanging nature of His purpose very clear to the heirs of what was promised, He confirmed it with an oath. God did this so that ... we who have fled to take hold of the hope offered to us may be greatly encouraged. (Hebrews 6:17–18)

God's promise of salvation to those who have faith in Christ Jesus and God's oath in Scripture confirming that promise will not change. They were the same yesterday, they are the same today, and they will remain the same tomorrow. As we face the uncertainty and challenges that the twenty-first century bring, God assures us that He will go forth with us into the new millennium just as He has led His people into every new century.

But what will the church of the twenty-first century face? God's Word assures us, "What has been will be again, what has been done will be done again; there is nothing new under the sun" (Ecclesiastes 1:9). Although the names have changed, the challenges the Christian church will face in the twenty-first century have not: idolatry (spirituality, mysticism, new age); attitude (postmodernism, modernism); witnessing to diverse cultures; growing churches; other religions; heresy; apathy; change. The Christian church has faced these same challenges since its beginning.

In this course we will identify some of the challenges Christians and the Christian church face as they move into the twenty-first century. We will seek guidance, comfort, counsel, and encouragement from God's Word—the unchanging source of all knowledge concerning life and salvation. We will have the opportunity to prepare ourselves for that which is here and is to come.

May God the Holy Spirit strengthen your faith as God's Word prepares you to face the challenges of the twenty-first century!

The Editors

1

MOVING DAY!

The old church downtown had been all I'd known. That was where my religion lived! When someone asked what religion I was, I could proudly point to that big old Gothic church with the tall steeple. "I'm Lutheran," I would say. But then the time came to move the congregation from the old sanctuary to a new building erected at a different location.

Sometime after the move, I drove by the old church building, which still sat empty. I remembered my confirmation day in that old building. I had received a Bible with my name printed on the cover. I had forgotten my tie and had to walk home to get it. I remembered the way the altar was set up. During Communion we passed behind the altar from one side to the other. Soon this old building would be torn down to make way for a new post office. I felt sad, as though somehow my religion was being changed or diminished.

The move was traumatic enough for some of the older church members. But tearing down the old building, which stood as a landmark just off the town square, seemed a sacrilege. Many came to realize that in moving from the old church to the new, they were making an even larger emotional move. They weren't changing their faith—just some of the "props" of their religion. But they found the change unsettling and threatening.

If we are honest with ourselves we must admit that we all have some concerns about change. Because we like to be in control, we feel threatened by change when it is thrust upon us. We worry that others will perceive us as unprogressive or "out of it" if we resist change. And, as people of God, we wonder what sweeping changes will mean as we live out our relationship with Him.

Many fear that taking a step forward in time means burning bridges to their past. But as we examine our life and the changes in how we live and interact with God and others, we also have new opportunities. We can reevaluate our ways of doing things by reaffirming the basic principles behind them.

I'VE GOT A THEORY!

A waiter at a small café in an industrial section of town was surprised on a quiet morning when a pastor wearing a traditional clerical collar sat down and ordered coffee. They had the following conversation:

Waiter: Will you have anything with your coffee this morning, sir?

Pastor: No, just coffee. Maybe a little conversation if you like. I'm waiting for a ride back to the airport.

Waiter: You're not from around here, are you?

Pastor: No. I'm from Minneapolis. Been in town for a meeting.

Waiter: What church you with?

Pastor: I'm a pastor of a Lutheran church back home in north Minneapolis.

Waiter: I'm Catholic myself. But I don't go much.

Pastor: Oh. Well, I guess you could say that I go a lot. *(Laughs)*

Waiter: Think you make up for me not going?

Pastor: Hardly. *(Thinks for a moment)* I can't even make up for myself.

Waiter: Say, I've got a theory. Mind if I test it out on you?

Pastor: Sure. Go ahead! I've got the time if you do!

Waiter: Great. *(Looks around and notes that there is no one else in the café)* I'm not real busy anyway. My theory is this. All religions are the same—they just look different from the outside.

Pastor: I'm not sure if I understand what you mean by "they just look different from the outside."

Waiter: We both worship God, you know, but we've got

priests, holy water, and lots of rituals. I don't know exactly, but you Lutherans don't have all those things, do you?

Pastor: Well, there are some similarities between the worship services of Lutherans and Catholics. After all, Martin Luther grew up and received his training within your Roman Catholic tradition. But what about other religions?

Waiter: What do you mean?

Pastor: There are a lot more differences between either of us and the Buddhist or Hindu faith. Are those religions all the same?

Waiter: *(Pauses and rubs his chin)* Well, I don't know much about Buddhism or Hinduism, but I suppose they're the same. They all believe in God, don't they?

Pastor: That's interesting. Technically, Buddhists don't believe in any kind of supreme being. Buddhists believe that peace comes from within and not from a supreme being outside ourselves. Hindus believe in many gods and find it difficult to describe any kind of inner peace at all.

Waiter: But religions are a lot alike. They all have religious people to lead them, buildings in which to hold their ceremonies, and some kind of faith, don't they?

Pastor: Sure. There are many religions in the world. And while they share certain similarities, there are many significant differences. But there are only two faiths—a faith in God and a faith in self.

Waiter: What do you mean?

Pastor: You asked before if I made up for you because I go to church multiple times each Sunday.

Waiter: And you said you can't even make up for yourself.

Pastor: Good, I'm glad you caught that. And that's right. Religion is a bunch of "dos" and "don'ts." And some people do better than others. But that doesn't make someone worthy or unworthy to get closer to God. Religion is a system of things that people construct to connect themselves back to God. On the other hand, faith is trust in the God who has made known Himself in the Scriptures.

Waiter: I don't get it.

Pastor: Did you ever learn that popular Bible verse recorded in John 3:16?

Waiter: Sure—that's the one people always hold up at football games, isn't it?

Pastor: Right. And do you know why they hold it up?

Waiter: No, why?

Pastor: Well, you tell me. What does it say?

Waiter: I'm not sure—remember, I'm not very religious, Father—I mean Pastor. But doesn't it start out, "For God so loved the world, that He gave His one and only Son ..."

Pastor: *(Finishing it)* "... that whoever believes in Him will not perish, but have eternal life."

Waiter: Yeah. That's it. *(Smiling)* Great. I remember!

Pastor: You remember—but do you believe?

Waiter: Believe what?

Pastor: Believe what it says?

Waiter: Why, sure I do. I just repeated it, didn't I?

Pastor: And that's the point. You can say the words—like going through the rituals and prayers in church. But does that mean you're going to heaven?

Waiter: Well, I surely hope so.

Pastor: But don't you think the God who literally owns and runs the universe would like to offer you more than hope? Look. *(Taking out his wallet)* If I were to give you this five-dollar bill, whose would it be?

Waiter: Yours?

Pastor: No. I said, if I gave it to you.

Waiter: You mean it would be mine, don't you?

Pastor: Exactly. And listen to that Bible verse from John 3:16: "God gave His one and only Son" so that if you believe, you will have eternal life. Eternal life is based not on what you have done but on what God has done for you in Jesus. Religion is what *you* have done—whether that be going or not going to church—like we were talking about before. But faith is believing and trusting that God has done everything necessary for us to have eternal life as a free gift.

Waiter: *(Thinking)* That's interesting.

Pastor: It's more than interesting. Even faith is God's gift to us.

MANY THEORIES—ONE TRUTH

There are numerous theories about God and the afterlife. You've no doubt heard many of them.

- Only members of certain religions will get into heaven.
- You have to lead a good and moral life to get into heaven.
- Only churchgoing people can expect to get into heaven.

Many believe, like the waiter in the café, that all religions are basically the same and that it doesn't matter what you believe as long as you are faithful to your beliefs. "God will honor any faithfulness," reasons the logical mind. "It doesn't matter which religious persuasion you happen to fall into by virtue of your cultural background or life experiences."

Christianity takes a different perspective. God's Word brings us a faith system based not on what we can do for God but rather on what God has done for us through His Son Jesus. Read the Bible verses in the margin and try to formulate your own "theory" about religion and faith.

Look, the Lamb of God, who takes away the sin of the world! John 1:29

He Himself bore our sins in His body on the tree, so that we might die to sins and live for righteousness; by His wounds you have been healed. 1 Peter 2:24

A SENSE OF CHANGE

Have you heard the story about the four blind people who went out to "see" an elephant? One encountered the trunk and exclaimed that the elephant was just like a hose. The next encountered an ear and said, "No. The elephant is just like a

For you know that it was not with perishable things such as silver or gold that you were redeemed from the empty way of life handed down to you from your forefathers, but with the precious blood of Christ, a lamb without blemish or defect. 1 Peter 1:18–19 fan!" The third blind person encountered the elephant's firm, stout leg and said that they both were wrong. "The elephant is like a tree!" The last laughed. He knew all the others were wrong. Grasping the elephant's tail, he insisted that the elephant was just like a rope!

Which one was right? Why, they all were, of course. But only from their own perspective. So how does this apply to religion and spirituality?

When Jesus was on trial, Pontius Pilate, in desperation, uttered a basic question: "What is truth?" Like others before and after him, Pilate thought that truth is relative—in the "eye of the beholder," so to speak. To illustrate this point, you might easily (but reluctantly!) answer questions about your weight or age. But scientists tell us that a person's weight and age change as that person travels faster and faster. Units of currency and the time of day vary from place to place too. Times and seasons change from one hemisphere to the other.

But God's Word assures us that our God doesn't change. "Jesus Christ is the same yesterday and today and forever" (Hebrews 13:8).

One of the greatest challenges facing the Christian church today is to selectively accept changes in style, form, and ritual without changing the message of our unchanging God. He always has and always will offer the gift of forgiveness and eternal life through His Son.

New Methods—Old Message

Stepping into the future does not have to mean burning bridges to our past. Just as God does not change, neither does His holy Word. It will continue to provide God's promises, encouragement, and comfort. It will continue to reveal God's truths to guide and direct us until we undergo the most dramatic change of all—one that transforms us from this world to the joy and bliss of heaven.

The tradition and practices help us to express our unity of our Christian heritage also as the people of God. Our liturgy gives us a common voice as the people of God. A pilgrim to the cave beneath the church built where Jesus was born was amazed to hear three different groups of people singing the same song, "Silent Night"—singing one song, but in different languages. When we encounter changes in worship and practice, we will seek to balance them with our heritage. The changes may be good, but we should not leave behind the rich Christian heritage all believers share.

TRADITION AND SCRIPTURE

Jesus' most ardent enemies, the Pharisees and the teachers of the law, seemed always to find fault with the way He did things. Jesus was an agent of change! When He healed a man with a crippled hand, the religious leaders accused Him of breaking God's Law, which they felt prohibited any work on the Sabbath. Jesus countered with a very simple question. "If any of you has a sheep and it falls into a pit on the Sabbath, will you not take hold of it and lift it out?" (Matthew 12:11).

"Therefore," Jesus concluded, "it is lawful to do good on the Sabbath." He also responded to the Pharisees with a quote from His Father: "I desire mercy, not sacrifice" (Matthew 12:7; quoting Hosea 6:6). Like the Pharisees, we may find ourselves "majoring in the minors"—acting like teachers of the law rather than practitioners of the Gospel.

When people condemned Jesus and His followers, He reminded them that their condemnation was an example of what God talked about through His prophet Isaiah: "These people honor Me with their lips, but their hearts are far from Me" (Matthew 15:8). By focusing on the meaning of our practices and making certain that they are in accord with God's Word, we can use creative approaches to meet our goals and objectives as the people of God.

Religion and Faith in the Twenty-First Century

Today we live in what some refer to as the postmodern era. Applied to religious life, postmodernism is characterized by the questioning of "old" truths, a dramatic decrease in loyalty to organizations or denominations, and truth-seeking in places considerably different from the traditional church.

Leonard Sweet, in his book *FaithQuakes* (Abingdon Press: Nashville, 1994), suggests that in the postmodern era, Christian churches must switch from "frog" evangelism to "lizard" evangelism. While frogs can sit and wait for their food—relying on their long and sticky tongues to collect supper—lizards actively search for their food.

In times past, many churches grew corresponding to the growth of member families and the community in which the church was located. Today, however, large families have become all but a relic of the past. Many churches are located in communities with little or no growth or with population loss. Nevertheless, the Great Commission remains: Jesus will have us reach out to the lost—to share the Good News so that the church may grow through the conversion of nonbelievers.

In order to effectively meet the needs of those who are new to the Christian faith, churches must engage in constant reexamination of their rituals and practices, determining which practices no longer work. To reach the lost, churches must take on the challenge of finding ways to appeal to a variety of people from a variety of backgrounds with a variety of spiritual needs.

Where There's Smoke, There's Fire!

A missionary once brought an American Indian chief to his new church. After a lengthy and spirited worship service, the missionary asked the chief what he thought about it. The chief pondered for a few moments. Then he gave his impression. "Big wind. Lotta dust. No rain!"

Perhaps the chief's assessment could be applied to many congregations today. Dramatic messages and emotional outbursts aren't necessarily signs of productive spiritual activity. Gains in membership by these means may only be incidental to the true mission of a church. The same can be said of congregations that successfully aim only at internal maintenance rather than outreach.

Congregations that are intentional about reaching the lost are made up of energized people with a mission. They focus on helping people see Christ. Energized people lived in Bible days too. One day John the Baptizer saw Jesus standing nearby. John did what Christians through the ages have been called to do. He pointed to Jesus. Then John spoke the immortal words, "Look, the Lamb of God, who takes away the sin of the world!" (John 1:29). If you believe as God's Word says, that you are a sinner forgiven by Jesus, neither the present nor the future threaten your faith. You have power not only to survive, but to thrive—power to sustain and power to proclaim His Word.

As members of the body of Christ and His church, we can boldly ask God to calm any fears we may have about the future of His church. He wants us to pray for spiritual strength and endurance as we cope with change, either supporting changes that glorify Him or resisting changes that undermine His will. Through His Word and Sacrament, the Holy Spirit will guide and encourage us as we proclaim the Gospel to people in future generations. The Spirit will also give us wisdom to understand the difference between unnecessary change and vital progress.

FOR DISCUSSION

1. What aspects of your religion have changed over the years?
   Do you use new hymnals or new forms of worship? Are you worshiping in a new building? What new leaders stand before you at worship? Do you wear different clothing to worship?

To what extent does your church use computers? Does your church use high-tech devices such as televisions, VCRs, and music synthesizers? Is your church on the World Wide Web? How many people within your church communicate through e-mail?

Do you offer multiple worship services in a variety of styles? How many small groups meet within ministries that didn't exist a few years ago? Has your faith changed with any of these changes?

2. How would you answer the waiter's question, "Can a pastor (or anyone else) who attends church regularly and frequently make up for someone else not going?" Can going to church save a person?

3. One writer, anxious to help church leaders keep current with the world, suggests that organizations ask the following questions of themselves. How would you answer?

   What is my role? As a church and a religious community, can we continue to expect our paid church staff to do most of the ministry, as was the case in the past? What can I do in service to Christ and others?

   What's my address? In what kind of community do we conduct ministry? What do I know about the culture in which I live and work that will help me to better serve acquaintances with the Gospel of Jesus Christ? Am I aware of any cultural overlaps that could help me to be a more effective messenger of Christ's message?

   Where am I headed? Many churches must leave the comfort of maintenance ministry and push out into the deep places of greater mission opportunity. Are you in a mission or do you live in a mission field?

   Whose church is my church? Is this Christ's church or mine? Does this church belong to a larger group such as a district, synod, or national church body, or does it belong to the people who live, work, and worship nearby?

4. Read John 4:1–26, the story of Jesus' conversation with the woman at the well. What was religion for this woman? How do you think she would describe faith? What do you think prompted her concerns in verse 9? Consider the age-old question "Which church is the right church?" as evidenced by her statement to Jesus in verse 20. If place isn't important for faith, what is?

5. If Jesus appeared right now, what questions would you ask Him? Do you think most people would ask about "religion" or "faith"?

6. For some people, the important thing about religion is what you eat or don't eat. How would you use Jesus' words in Matthew 15:11, "What goes into a man's mouth does not make him 'unclean,' but what comes out of his mouth, that is what makes him 'unclean,' " to explain your beliefs in the following situations?

   • The first time one of the young people played a guitar during a worship service, several old members vowed that it would never happen again. "God always intended that we use an organ to accompany our music. Why change now?"

- The church council agreed that it was important to be welcoming and inviting when new people visited the church. But on Monday morning in the coffee shop, several individuals who had visited agreed that it was the coldest church they ever attended. "Most of those people were too busy talking to family and friends to greet us after church. The only person who talked to us was the pastor!" the visitors exclaimed.
- Due to concern about the spread of disease, someone suggested that the church abandon the common cup for wine in Holy Communion. One man stood up and exclaimed, "It's more important to maintain the one cup than to be concerned about what's in it."
- One church decided to invite women to be ushers, and three families quit because, as they said, "Women are to keep silent in the church!"

7. What changes has your church encountered in recent years? What changes are likely to face your church in the future? What can you do to help your church meet these changes in a God-pleasing way? If "we've never done it that way before," how can we make a smooth transition without driving people away? What can we change and what can't we change?

2

RELIGION AND SPIRITUALITY

WHAT HAVE YOU CHANGED TODAY?

If you were to list the most significant events in your life, what would they be? Birth, Baptism, confirmation, marriage, the birth of a child, the 15 minutes of glory when you made the game-winning free throw? When the story of your life is finally written, what will really count?

What about the most significant events in the history of your community? The big fire? The election of a famous person to high office?

What would you list as the most significant events in the history of the United States? The Civil War, the election of certain presidents, or the passing of certain laws? When the final history books are written, what will really count?

Although the twenty-first century doesn't begin until 2000, most people eagerly await that day when they must change all of the numbers to write the year—not just the last one or two! Other people fear that date because they think the world will come to a sudden end. Still others wonder if computers will fail to compute and aircraft will fall from the sky.

Often people fear change because they can't predict how much will change. Since they can't control their future, they prefer to stay the same. And yet very little stays the same. Changes take place all around us. The only exception is God. He doesn't change. So in response to all these changes, we pray with the hymn writer, "O Thou who changest not, abide with me."

In a memorable conversation between the judge Samuel and King Saul of Israel, the wise judge confronted Saul with his unfaithfulness and God's changeless faithfulness. "Why did you not obey the Lord?" Samuel asked. Saul, seeking to justify himself—and hoping for a change in God's will—protested, "I did obey the Lord."

Samuel stood his ground and explained how God operates. "He who is the Glory of Israel does not lie or change His mind; for He is not a man, that He should change His mind" (1 Samuel 15:29). During their conversation Saul confessed, "I have sinned. I violated the LORD's command and your instructions. I was afraid of the people and so I gave in to them" (15:24).

Again, through the prophet Malachi, God says, "I the LORD do not change" (Malachi 3:6). Because God doesn't change, He expects us to repent and change. He expects us to turn away from evil and do His will. He expects us to become more childlike.

Once, Jesus held a little child and said, "Unless you change and become like little children, you will never enter the kingdom of heaven" (Matthew 18:3). Jesus further explained what He meant by suggesting that we become like little children: "Therefore, whoever humbles himself like this child is the greatest in the kingdom of heaven" (Matthew 18:4). God doesn't change, but He expects us to change completely!

Consider other big changes that will occur or that have already occurred in your lifetime. You probably get the news or communicate with people differently than you did 5 or 10 years ago. Some of you regularly use a fax machine, video, and the Internet. You are likely to use computers in your work and at home or when you drive your car. Life would be noticeably different if you suddenly discontinued using these devices.

Perhaps things have changed in your religious life too. You may go to church more or less often when compared to your parents. Since the days of your youth, it's likely that the music, the worship service, and perhaps even the style of sermons have changed. What about the way you practice your religious faith? Do you pray every day? Read the Bible regularly? Talk to others about your faith?

Do you have a support group of Christian friends with whom you can discuss your doubts, fears, and failures? With whom do you celebrate your successes and share your joys? For many, experiences like these make up the "church" of today. But some people never go.

Just because people don't go to church doesn't mean they aren't religious or spiritual. It just means they don't go to church. They may choose to worship God in a different way. They may worship, but they may not worship the true God. Some people are more spiritual, but they may not be religious. There is a difference. How would "spirituality" look different from "religiousness"?

Consider the results of a recent survey of "unchurched" people:

- 74 percent said, "There is no value in attending organized worship services."
- 81 percent said, "Churches have too many problems."
- 48 percent agreed they didn't have enough time to go to church.
- 40 percent felt churches asked for money too often.
- 36 percent said, "Church services are boring."
- 34 percent said, "Church services are irrelevant to the way I live."
- 12 percent said, "I don't believe in God" or "I am unsure that God actually exists."

With even a passing knowledge of Christianity, you could write a rebuttal to each of these statements; however, the church must examine the underlying motivations of these people if it is to positively affect them in the twenty-first century. What are they really saying? What do these survey results say to you? What do they convey to the Christian church? Are there changes that the church must make? Has your congregation considered any of these questions?

You Can Have Any Color You Want—As Long As It's Black

In the early days of this century, Henry Ford pioneered the low-cost automobile. He mass-produced a vehicle that almost everyone could afford and instantly generated a huge market. But some say he held on too long to his one-model, one-color, high-volume car strategy. Eventually, General Motors came along, offered variety, and captured some of Ford's market.

GM offered automobiles that came in a variety of colors. Soon they were producing slightly higher-priced vehicles, and they offered something new: consumer financing. But GM, too, held on to their plan too long. While they enjoyed some success by combining their new strategies with Ford's ideas of mass production and affordability, vehicle quality began to suffer. Soon other manufacturers capitalized on these errors. The story could go on and on.

What changes do you believe churches have made that compare to offering automobiles in different colors? What is God saying to His people about the way they celebrate His presence in the world and in the church today? What changes can Christians encourage without sacrificing quality and integrity? Do you think that having many different translations of the Bible enhances or stifles the growth of the church? These questions are worth discussion. In addition to the usual church-meeting topics, perhaps they should appear on the agenda!

Confessing to the One We Can Neither See nor Touch!

The great apostle Paul traveled to the city of Athens. He noticed that the city was full of idols—images of many different gods that the people believed could exert power over their lives and help them. As was his custom, Paul entered one of the Jewish synagogues seeking a "spiritual" discussion. He knew the synagogue was a place where he could talk to people about religious or spiritual matters and they would understand. We don't know exactly what he said there, but we do know from other conversations that he talked about worshiping God and having faith in the one God who raised His Son from the dead.

Because listeners found Paul's message to be foreign and confusing, they invited him to the place where they often interrogated visiting foreign leaders—the Areopagus, or Mars Hill. Paul's listeners functioned like teachers or censors in their society. They listened to new ideas, and then they decided if others should be allowed to hear those ideas.

Paul stood up in the middle of their meeting on the Areopagus and said,

> Men of Athens! I see that in every way you are very religious. For as I walked around and looked carefully at your objects of worship, I even found an altar with this inscription: TO AN UNKNOWN GOD. Now what you worship as something unknown I am going to proclaim to you. The God who made the world and everything in it is the Lord of heaven and earth and does not live in temples built by hands. ... He has set a day when He will judge the world with justice by the Man He has appointed. He has given proof of this to all men by raising Him from the dead. (Acts 17:22–31)

At this mention of a supernatural miracle—especially a resurrection from the dead—some of them sneered, but some wanted to hear more about it. Scripture says that some of them even became followers of the Christ. What is important is that whenever Paul wanted to share his faith in Christ, he went to a place where spiritual people gathered. He knew they would listen.

Our society has its modern monuments to unknown gods too. People gather at these places seeking answers to questions or ways to fulfill empty lives. Such gathering places are rarely churches. Therefore, churches must determine what these monuments are and where they exist. Our churches may need to take their message "on the road" as Paul did.

WHAT DOES IT MEAN TO BE SPIRITUAL?

When Jesus walked this earth, He observed how people treated each other. Some were kind and gentle; others were vicious and violent. Both kinds of people claimed to be religious and believe in God. So Jesus challenged them: "A new command I give you: Love one another. As I have loved you, so you must love one another. By this all men will know that you are My disciples, if you love one another" (John 13:34–35). At another time Jesus said, "Greater love has no one than this, that he lay down his life for his friends" (John 15:13).

Jesus compared Himself to a sacrificial shepherd and His people to sheep. "I am the good shepherd; I know My sheep and My sheep know Me—just as the Father knows Me and I know the Father—and I lay down My life for the sheep" (John 10:14–15). To be spiritual is to live consistent with what you profess and confess about Jesus.

James said that faith without works is dead. "If anyone considers himself religious and yet does not keep a tight rein on his tongue, he deceives himself and his religion is worthless. Religion that God our Father accepts as pure and faultless is this: to look after orphans and widows in their distress and to keep oneself from being polluted by the world" (James 1:26–27). And we read in Matthew 7:16, "By their fruit you will recognize them."

These Scriptures have confused many and generated numerous discussions. We believe, as Paul says, that we are saved entirely by God's grace and not by our deeds, however good they might be. "For it is by grace you have been saved, through faith—and this not from yourselves, it is the gift of God—not by works, so that no one can boast" (Ephesians 2:8–9). We can do nothing to save ourselves. Jesus suggests that our good works or fruits of faith simply identify but don't create faith. "There is no difference, for all have sinned and fall short of the glory of God, and are justified freely by His grace through the redemption that came by Christ Jesus" (Romans 3:22–24).

Which is more important—to be spiritual or religious? Our definition of being "religious" would probably include going to church, reading the Bible, and praying. But as you look at the previous Bible verses, do you get the idea that being spiritual is even more important? Perhaps being spiritual could be defined as "relating to others as if you were relating to God." Or "doing good to others as if you were doing good to God." Jesus originated what is popularly called the Golden Rule when He said, "So in everything, do to others what you would have them do to you, for this sums up the Law and the Prophets" (Matthew 7:12).

Jesus changed our spiritual nature, and His changes require some self-examination. How do you identify troublesome people? How do you react to them? According to John, the great love of God, shown in Jesus Christ, ought to give us strength to overcome evil with goodness and love (John 4:4). But there is more to this issue.

Some people insist that they do treat others nicely, but Jesus still condemns their religion as exclusive and discriminatory. "You have heard that it was said, 'Love your neighbor and hate your enemies.' But I tell you: Love your enemies and pray for those who persecute you. ... If you love those who love you, what reward will you get? Are not even the tax collectors doing that? And if you greet only your brothers, what are you doing more than others? Do not even pagans do that? Be perfect, therefore, as your heavenly Father is perfect" (Matthew 5:43–48). Many strive for religious perfection. But God, in His grace, loves us and teaches us how to be perfect in love and forgiveness.

"LOVE EACH OTHER AS I HAVE LOVED YOU" (JOHN 15:12)

"If anyone gives even a cup of cold water to one of these little ones because he is My disciple, I tell you the truth, he will certainly not lose his reward" (Matthew 10:42). Have you been blessed by these words from Jesus? In His picture of Judgment Day, Jesus seems focused on good works—things people do— and yet He calls those gathered at His right hand "blessed." The dilemma comes in connecting our "doing" with God's free blessings. The connection comes in this: we have the gift of faith, and now, operating out of faith, we respond with good works that glorify God.

As Jesus did, we constantly meet people who say they are religious but who don't love others and therefore act as if they don't belong to God. Are we to condemn them? Perhaps, by their lack of love, they condemn themselves. "We love because He first loved us. If anyone says, 'I love God,' yet hates his brother, he is a liar. For anyone who does not love his brother, whom he has seen, cannot love God, whom he has not seen. And He has given us this command: Whoever loves God must also love his brother" (1 John 4:19–21).

Being spiritual, then, is more than being religious. It means showing our faith in and love for God by the way we treat others.

As churches change, it will become more important to look beyond labels and express our faith in spiritual rather than religious terms.

I'M SITTING ON TOP OF THE WORLD

What goals do you have for your life? Are you striving for more money or a better house or car?

People often think of goals in physical terms, characterized by things they can see, touch, taste, and feel. We want to sit on top of the world. We want to have enough to take life easy. But what about spiritual goals—things we can't see and touch? What about having things like peace of mind, friends you can trust, and a rich prayer and devotional life? What about giving glory to God and helping others?

A most worthy goal is humility. Jesus frequently spoke

about humbling ourselves and taking the "lowest place" (Luke 14:10). Jesus—God Himself—came to be a servant and give His life as a ransom for us (Matthew 20:28). In God's view, humility brings meaning to life and gives substance to spirituality. Humility means adopting the role of a willing servant. But eventually, our time available to serve will expire.

Jesus told a story about a man who thought he had everything, and then his harvest came in better than he had ever imagined. He didn't have space to store all that he had, so he began to build bigger barns. Jesus called him a "fool" and said that because he was going to die that night, his bigger barns and all the things he could put into them wouldn't make any difference. He was a fool, not because he wanted a bigger barn, but because he hadn't placed the physical "things" of life in proper perspective to spiritual things—like the end of life and the opportunity to glorify God and serve others.

I KNOW THE ANSWER— WHAT WAS THE QUESTION?

After listening to a number of questions, a young Sunday school student realized that all the questions had the same answer: "Jesus." She exclaimed, "I know what the next answer is. What is the question?"

What questions do you have about your own spirituality? "I know where I'm going—do you?" That's an important question for everyone to answer.

Have you ever entered a room and forgotten what you came for? You probably returned to where you started before you could remember your original mission. Have you ever backed out of the driveway and, because of habit, gone in the wrong direction because you failed to concentrate on where you were going? Christians need to concentrate on where they are going. Thanks to God, we have our answer. Jesus died on the cross to take away our sins and give direction to our lives. Because of what Jesus did, we're headed in the right direction despite our frequent detours and our need to repeatedly start over.

Spirituality is more than "going through the motions." It is a connectedness. It is a belonging. Spirituality is seeking to connect with God as we are connected to others. Spirituality is seeing God's glory in the world around us (Psalm 19:1) and the people He has given us to share His world.

In the 1980s, people were concerned about "things"—materialism. In the 1990s, people seemed more concerned about spirituality, though not always Christianity. What's next for spirituality? Will people be more involved in a mixture of religions or a reduction of spiritual matters to the lowest common denominator? Will paganism proliferate? Will social action and justice become more important than worship or small-group support? These questions will eventually have answers— answers that will impact spirituality as well as religion.

SUNDAY MORNING CHRISTIANS?

Some churches fight change. Mark Twain once said, "Even if you are on the right track, you'll get run over if you just sit there." How do you think these words are prophetic for the church of the twenty-first century?

The church is changing, and if we don't get out of the way, we may be run over. Church isn't just for Sunday anymore. In fact, some people never come to their church buildings on Sunday. Other days or nights of the week are more in keeping with their work and leisure schedules. Some may argue that the church shouldn't conform to the world, and this is true. But what changes can be made to accommodate a changing world without changing the main message of God's love in Christ?

TELLING STORIES

A church consultant said that the church today "has to do with how people think and arrange information. We are moving from a world in which people primarily learned by proposition, proclamation, and rational presentation to a world in which the primary learning mode is narrative storytelling" (Leadership Network, "Net Fax," no. 92).

You and your church have narratives. You can identify these narratives by recalling events that "define" your spiritual existence. The following questions may help you determine the substance of your narratives:

- Do people talk about what happened at a Baptism, or is the voters' meeting a more likely topic?
- What was it like when someone came into your church building for the very first time?
- What was it like when that person, who had resisted God for so many years, finally received Christ's love and became a spiritual person centered on God rather than on self?

These are some narratives that will shape the church and spirituality of the future.

We can't confine spirituality to Sunday morning. People are looking for spiritual answers seven days a week. In his book *FaithQuakes*, the pastor and church futurist Leonard Sweet quotes Dr. David O. Wiebers, Chair of the Scientific Advisory Council of the Humane Society of the United States. He says, "Perhaps the time has come for all of us to recognize that humankind's greatest goal, which outweighs lengthening of life through medical advancements, is to evolve spiritually."

SPIRITUALITY—OUR LINK BACK TO GOD

Have you ever thought of what it would have been like to live with God in the Garden of Eden? The old hymn suggests, "And He walks with me, and He talks with me, and He tells me that I am His own." Wouldn't that be great?

What if the church were more like that? What if the church were a place where people heard God talk, where they experienced God walking with them, and where they came to know that they belonged to Him? What's keeping you from experiencing those kinds of things—and not just within the walls of a particular building or on the grounds of an institutional campus?

One phenomenon of the institutional church of the 1980s and 1990s is something called "meta-church." Meta is a Greek word which means "like," "similar to," or "beyond," suggesting some change or improvement. Meta-churches recognize a spirituality that is beyond buildings, programs, and scheduled activities.

Many growing churches have developed a number of small groups that reflect the "meta" concept. These groups are variously described as activity, study, and project groups. Regardless of their task or goal, these small groups often include the elements of study, nurture, and support. They are, however, more than study groups. They are more than prayer groups. They are more than support groups.

These groups focus on community and growth. Some even suggest leaving "an empty chair" in the group to emphasize the need for growth. When growth is anticipated, the group prays about who will join them. And when a group grows beyond 8 or 10 people, it trains a new leader, and like many-celled organisms, the group divides and grows again.

Some churches borrow from the popular 12-step model pioneered by Alcoholics Anonymous. They use the same model of "powerlessness" and reliance on a "higher power" as AA, but they consciously include an explicitly Christian approach to healing, recovery, and growth in a variety of human trauma. Twelve-step groups, as an approach to spirituality, regularly appear on the calendar of events of many churches and communities.

A visit to any popular bookstore will disclose another spiritual movement that may or may not be Christian or even religious in nature. The so-called "self-help" movement is popular. Books of "how-to" techniques and programs are applied to areas such as parenting, investing, dieting, and healthy living. Often these techniques suggest that help can come from within. But Christians recognize that, despite the power of the individual, the strongest power in the universe comes from God in Christ.

FROM GENERATION TO GENERATION

Management guru Peter Drucker often lends his considerable insight and skill to spiritual matters and to the changing church. He says,

> The biggest issue in every developed country in the next 25 years is not rich or poor, but the relationship between young and old. Changing demographics, a shift in the working population and the explosion of urban concentrations of people combine to create a new world in which the traditional church will not work. The emergence of the pastoral church, one which focuses on the congregation and the individual within the congregation, has to be the most important social development in this country in the last 20–25 years. Pastoral churches see their congregation as a resource, not a market; the communicant not as a customer, but a partner. (*NEXT,* Jan.–Feb. 1998)

"Lord, you have been our dwelling place throughout all generations. Before the mountains were born or You brought forth the earth and the world, from everlasting to everlasting You are God" (Psalm 90:2).

FOR DISCUSSION

1. What changes have you made today? What future changes do you anticipate in your lifetime? How do you expect the future will change the way you relate to God and others around you?
2. How do you connect being saved by grace through faith (Ephesians 2:8–9) and Jesus' words in Matthew 25:40—"Whatever you did for one of the least of these brothers of Mine, you did for Me"? Do Jesus' words conflict with James 2:17?
3. Compare your definition of spirituality with the scriptural concept. Or, to make the task easier, complete this sentence: "I know that a person is spiritual when this person does and says the following ..."
   Now check Scripture. Read James 3. What does such a small thing as your tongue have to do with being spiritual? Now read 1 John, chapters 3 and 4, and write down some observable evidence that you believe would help to identify a spiritual person.
4. How do you think the way people relate spiritually is changing and will be different in the twenty-first century?

5. What does "spiritual" mean to you as you consider being God's servant and having a limited amount of time in which to do it?
6. What style of leadership will the church need in the future? In the 1980s, pastors were often like the CEO of a large company. In the 1990s, church staffs sought to work more as a team. What will the future bring?
7. Martin Luther pioneered the idea of "the priesthood of all believers." Why do you think this mobilization of the laity will be more important in the church of the future?
8. If you belong to a church that publishes a calendar of events, study that calendar. How many of the activities listed didn't exist a few years ago? How many of the activities are for members, and how many are designed to reach out into your community?
9. How about your church's budget? What portion of the finances are spent to help maintain the organization, and what is left over to reach out to those who don't confess Jesus as Lord and Savior?
10. Think about all the changes that we have talked about in this chapter on spirituality versus religion. What implications for the future do you see in Drucker's quote? What are the implications for organized religions around you? For your church (if you belong to one)? And how can you jump on the bandwagon, rather than stand in the middle of the road waiting to be run over?

3

A New Time—A New Thing (Postmodernism)

All Things New?

In a vision, the apostle John saw the peacefulness of heaven. He took comfort in seeing Jesus, the Lamb, sitting on His throne. And he heard some very encouraging news. Of his vision of heaven, John tells us, "He who was seated on the throne said, 'I am making everything new!' " (Revelation 21:5). "Really? Everything new?" you might ask. "Everything? Must I change my faith too?"

The word "new" occurs frequently in Scriptures. God talks about a new heaven and a new earth. He talks of a new covenant or promise with His people. He talks about being new or "renewed" in Christ. But everything new? What are we to do—discard the old? Is it not important to keep any of the old?

Should we throw out our Bibles and choose some other book or computer software as our supreme authority? Do modern times call for a new god? On the contrary. Jesus Christ is always the same. One of God's foremost characteristics is that He doesn't change. We can count on that. In words that might come from a modern conversation, "You can take that to the bank!" Or in words that might be more comforting, "You can count on His unchangeableness—right up to the gates of heaven!" Perhaps the best words are "Be faithful, even to the point of death, and I will give you the crown of life" (Revelation 2:10). "God was reconciling the world to Himself in Christ, not counting men's sins against them" (2 Corinthians 5:19).

That message will never change. But the language and the style by which it comes to us may change.

Think of the changes you have experienced in your lifetime. Now think of the changes your church and religion have undergone. Has your religion changed? What about the color of the hymnal, the decorations inside the building in which you worship, or the clothing styles of those leading or participating in worship? Have those changes affected your relationship with God? In the words of the hymn writer, we say, "O Thou who changes not, abide with me!" God, through all the changes of my life, please remain the one constant that I can count on!

A DIFFERENT WAY OF LOOKING AT THINGS

Optical illusions can be fun for some but frustrating for others. For example, at first glance, some of the newer "Ultra 3-D" pictures appear to be nothing more than a jumble of random shapes and colors. After staring intently at one for a few moments, some people see the "hidden" picture. But, unfortunately, others continue to stare at the "surface" presentation and get frustrated because they can't see or don't perceive the hidden message. Some have suggested it's the angle at which you view these pictures that helps. It's like a secret password that some have and some don't. Fun for some but frustrating for others!

God's Word, the Bible, can be like that. Once, when Jesus was teaching, His disciples didn't understand Him and asked what His parables meant. He replied, "The knowledge of the secrets of the kingdom of God has been given to you, but to others I speak in parables, so that 'though seeing, they may not see; though hearing, they may not understand' " (Luke 8:10).

One person made the point of Luke 8:10 this way (although it isn't the most polite way of initiating a witnessing opportunity). When an unbeliever expressed frustration in not understanding God's meaning in a particular Bible passage, this person said, "That's what you get for reading other people's mail!" Perhaps witnessing your faith in Christ could be seen as sharing and explaining your "mail." Are there some "secrets" or "inside information" that you need to reveal before other people can understand what your Friend has written?

The church is changing its way of doing things, but the message of the Gospel of Christ will never change. The password will never change either. Faith will always unlock the secrets of Scripture.

MODERN AND POSTMODERN

Those who study and promote the growth of churches have come to call our era "postmodern." They label people born in the 1920s, '30s, and early '40s as the "Builders." The generation born from the mid-'40s to the mid-'60s is called "Baby Boomers," or simply "Boomers." These generations were born during the so-called "modern" era. The two generations born immediately after that are popularly called "postmodern" and include the "Baby Busters," or "Generation X," born from 1964 to 1984, and the "Millennials," born after 1984.

So what's the difference? Why would Christians and the church be concerned about differences in people—especially in the way they perceive spirituality? People born before 1964 seem to have a different view of spiritual matters. Study the following list of characteristics of modern and postmodern thinking as suggested by one author. Do you agree or disagree, and why? With these differences in mind, what changes in style or approach could you make in order to more effectively share your faith in Christ?

Modern	Postmodern
Skeptical	Spiritual
Enjoy the "natural" world	Rediscovering "supernatural" world
Automatically accept rational authority	Open to alternative authorities

| Believe history is progressive | Disillusioned with history |
| Trained in "the Scientific Method" | Immersed in "information" revolution |

(Leadership Network, "Net Fax," no. 88)

You Shall Be My Witnesses

Has anyone asked if you would testify as a witness to an auto accident? Jesus asked His disciples to testify as witnesses, but what they saw was no accident. Just before He left earth, Jesus gathered His disciples on a hillside near Jerusalem and began speaking to them. As they were watching, He was lifted up until a cloud hid Him from their sight. His parting words were, "And you will be My witnesses in Jerusalem, and in all Judea and Samaria, and to the ends of the earth" (Acts 1:8).

Jesus could have been uneasy, leaving earth and His young church in the hands of inexperienced and frightened people. During His three years in close relationship with them, one betrayed Him into the hands of His enemies, one denied knowing Jesus at all, and several others wanted to call down fire from heaven to burn up anyone who refused to believe. But Jesus knew His followers would soon change. They would receive the power of God's Holy Spirit, who would help them in His absence. Jesus set up His church to grow, and He knew that it wouldn't and shouldn't remain the same.

Outreach Methodology

A generation ago, popular evangelism and outreach programs centered on door-to-door "cold calling." Groups of people would canvas a neighborhood, asking questions about church involvement and hoping to share faith in Jesus Christ with individuals who opened their doors. But today, people cherish their privacy. In many areas, the days of knocking on doors and sharing Christ's love is gone. Many people resent that intrusion.

Another popular evangelism tool, the "mass rally" approach popularized by Billy Graham, has also diminished in effectiveness. Once, people would gather in large groups and listen to a rational and emotional appeal. Some would come forward to make a "decision" to follow Christ. Today, it seems that people are less willing to attend large group meetings unless they wholly support the cause before they make the commitment.

Some people know more about popular evangelists than they do about God's Word. While the Holy Bible is still the best-selling book in the world, it appears that people know and accept less and less of what is actually contained in the Bible. For example, a recent survey by Barna Associates revealed that 58 percent of 11,000 people surveyed didn't know that Jesus first spoke the Sermon on the Mount. Some thought that Graham did!

As a Christian, how would you respond to someone who didn't know that Jesus preached the Sermon on the Mount? What's your feeling about someone who doesn't believe that Jesus rose from the dead? According to Barna's survey, 50 percent of those surveyed don't believe that Jesus physically rose from the dead.

It's one thing to deal with biblically illiterate people and quite another to deal with people who don't believe even the basic tenets of Christianity. In this postmodern era, Christian churches that wish to remain faithful to God's Great Commission must commit themselves to find ways of reaching not only biblically illiterate Christians, but unbelievers as well.

God has called us to be witnesses. He didn't really offer us a choice, and He didn't say it would be easy! The most effective method of sharing your faith remains a reliable constant: a personal and one-on-one witnessing to the wonderful things that God has done in your life.

Churches that have experienced numerical growth within the past decade report that the most effective method of reaching out to others is still by inviting family, friends, and acquaintances to worship. Another effective option is to take them to a small prayer or study group. Use the network of family and friends that you already have to reach others for Jesus Christ.

ARE YOU SAVED, BROTHER?

A popular cartoon shows a man walking a street corner and carrying a sign that reads "The end is near." He accosts a passerby and, grabbing him by the shirt collar, demands, "Repent or be damned."

Some still try strong-arm methods of converting people. These are contrary to any biblical models of evangelism and, from a practical standpoint, are largely ineffective anyway. If God doesn't force anyone to accept saving faith, neither should those who are determined to save others by force do so. Besides, Christians have a power beyond muscle and tough rhetoric. They have prayer! They also have patience, self-control, gentleness, and other fruit of the Spirit (Galatians 5:22–23).

Christians need effective means to approach outreach and evangelism. Congregations need to examine the nature of their worship and social gatherings in light of what attracts people today. (This may even be a technological twist on Paul's speaking in places where people were known to gather!) But should we seek to perpetuate the institution of the church and be less concerned about the spiritual truths the church teaches and confesses?

As biblical Christians, we answer a resounding "no." But we must realize that some things are changing. Change is the order of the day. There isn't a huge market for manual typewriters and black-and-white televisions anymore. But once there was! Our "tools" for presenting the message become quickly outdated—only the message is always relevant. After all, "Jesus Christ is the same yesterday and today and forever" (Hebrews 13:8).

LIVING IN AN ERA OF THE BIGGEST SOCIAL EARTHQUAKE IN HISTORY

Postmodernism is certainly a factor to reckon with when reaching out with the Gospel of Jesus Christ. We are "living in one of the biggest social earthquakes in the history of the world" (Leonard Sweet, *FaithQuakes*, p. 9). We already accept that the Gospel does not and cannot change. The message of Christ crucified cannot and will not ever change. But the way it is conveyed must and will change. To distinguish the message from the medium, we plead, "God, grant us the wisdom to know the difference!"

God provides many wonderful assurances that His church will always exist on earth and that He will preserve in faith those who come to Him and remain in Him. "My sheep listen to My voice; I know them, and they follow Me. I give them eternal life, and they shall never perish; no one can snatch them out of My hand. My Father, who has given them to Me, is greater than all; no one can snatch them out of My Father's hand" (John 10:27–29).

YOU HAVE HEARD THAT IT WAS SAID ... BUT I SAY TO YOU!

Jesus recognized a need to change the way of looking at things. In His well-known Sermon on the Mount, Jesus explained how He was changing the model or paradigm for looking at the church and church authority. As examples, He used several of the Ten Commandments given to Moses on Mount Sinai. People already knew them well. For centuries their rabbis had studied and interpreted them. Jesus carefully upheld the law of Moses. Then He offered a "Spirit-motivated" interpretation, which reflected the kind and loving heart of His Father.

Several times Jesus began His teaching by saying, "You have heard that it was said … ," and then concluded by adding, "but I say to you … !" For example, He said, "You have heard that it was said, 'You shall not commit adultery.' But I say to you that everyone who looks at a woman with lust has already committed adultery with her in his heart" (Matthew 5:27–28).

Without using our sociological terms, Jesus pointed out the difference between "modern" and "postmodern" thinking. The strict letter of the Law requires immediate retribution; the postmodern Christian seeks to learn a person's motivation and how best to approach that person with the Law of God and the Gospel of a forgiving and accepting Christ.

We who live in the "mission fields" of current society are ready to hear God's Word and answer His clear call. Jesus invites, even commands us to pray that the Lord of the harvest will give us clear direction about how to share a spiritual message with people living in the twenty-first century. "The harvest is plentiful but the workers are few" (Matthew 9:37).

All this talk about new methods and new styles for witnessing hasn't changed the basic message. Paul reminds us that "if anyone is in Christ, he is a new creation; the old has gone, the new has come!" (2 Corinthians 5:17).

After a recent storm in the Midwest, insurance adjusters stood in one family's yard discussing what would become of their home, which was badly damaged. The homeowners said they couldn't live in the house because the roof had been blown away. It was too dangerous even to reenter their home to salvage their undamaged belongings. What roof was left was hanging precariously above their family car. The town authorities were ready to condemn the structure. But the insurance company was debating whether or not to repair the house!

Would you want to live in a condemned home? Finally, the property owner said in exasperation, "We got the best insurance policy we could buy. Why don't you just total it, get on with things, and build us a new home?" Wouldn't you say the same of your God and your faith in Him? "We've got the best there is. Why not just condemn sin and get on with life in Christ? Why not begin all over—become new in Christ?" That's the unchanging message that God presents to us and encourages us to somehow perpetuate.

A PROMISE OF FORGIVENESS

No one would deny that many changes are happening in our world today. Violence seems to be the rule rather than the exception in almost every land on earth. Homicide, assassinations, and road rage are common news events nearly every day. People call for justice and equality among the races. People react legally and economically, but what about spiritually? What "spiritual" response can you offer when someone is senselessly killed, whether deliberately or accidentally? Christians can't simply wring their hands in helplessness. Christians respond with hope and forgiveness. And when it comes to God's forgiveness, there is really nothing new. He offers a "new covenant" that is quite old.

Thousands of years ago, God made this promise:

"The time is coming," declares the LORD, "when I will make a new covenant with the house of Israel and with the house of Judah. It will not be like the covenant I made with their forefathers when I took them by the hand to lead them out of Egypt, because they broke My covenant, though I was a husband to them. ... This is the covenant I will make with the house of Israel after that time. ... I will put My law in their minds and write it on their hearts. I will be their God, and they will be My people. No longer will a man teach his neighbor, or a man his brother, saying, 'Know the LORD,' because they will all know Me, from the least of them to the greatest. ... For I will forgive their wickedness and will remember their sins no more." (Jeremiah 31:31–34)

Many years ago, when God delivered His people at the Red Sea, His musicians reminded the people that "some trust in chariots and some in horses, but we trust in the name of the LORD our God" (Psalm 20:7).

Modern society trusts in information. Computers have contributed to a glut of information, especially through the "online" phenomenon. Some people think that if there is a problem, you can just throw a little more money or a lot of information at the difficulty and it will simply go away. Actually, the simple Gospel of Jesus Christ is the answer for every situation. We need to learn new and different ways to apply God's message of grace. "Such confidence as this is ours through Christ before God. Not that we are competent in ourselves to claim anything for ourselves, but our competence comes from God. He has made us competent as ministers of a new covenant—not of the letter but of the Spirit; for the letter kills, but the Spirit gives life" (2 Corinthians 3:4–6).

This so-called "postmodern" era may have different ways of viewing spirituality, but Christians will always respond with the life and hope that only God gives. And we don't claim to have figured this out by ourselves, either. God is the one who first talked about a new covenant—a new way of looking at Christ for a new era.

The changes that churches face today are not new either. Remember this story?

> John's disciples came and asked Him [Jesus], "How is it that we and the Pharisees fast, but Your disciples do not fast?" Jesus answered, "How can the guests of the bridegroom mourn while he is with them? The time will come when the bridegroom will be taken from them; then they will fast. No one sews a patch of unshrunk cloth on an old garment, for the patch will pull away from the garment, making the tear worse. Neither do men pour new wine into old wineskins. If they do, the skins will burst, the wine will run out and the wineskins will be ruined. No, they pour new wine into new wineskins, and both are preserved." (Matthew 9:14–17)

Have you experienced similar questions or disagreements in a church or other organization? Have you witnessed controversies over worship form or music style? How do we honor the needs of different groups of people at the same time as we honor Christ's Gospel of forgiveness and love for all people? This is one of the biggest challenges facing Christians and the church today. Like it or not, you may be right in the center of this problem. Has Christ called you to respond? How and when?

Let's look at all this once more. Not everyone is enthralled with the whole idea of postmodernism. Some urge caution when using sociological terms and ideas to interpret the mission of the church. Os Guinness, in his book *Dining with the Devil* (Baker Book House Company, 1993), adds as a subtitle "The Megachurch Movement Flirts with Modernity." Listen to and think about what Guinness says in his introduction.

> My purpose is not to discuss this vital movement, or even to assess it comprehensively from a theological perspective, but to critique the perils and pitfalls that come from the 'new ground.' ... My approach is to examine trends, raise issues, and set out principles so that we may engage with this vital movement with our eyes open and our ears alert, being as self-critical and discerning as the gospel requires. Of course, I am aware that at the end of the day what I think about the church growth movement or anything else matters little. What really matters is what God thinks. For the day is coming when we will either hear "Well done," and our work will prove to be "gold and silver." Or we will be judged by the test of fire and our work show up as "wood, hay, and stubble." Or, worst of all, we may hear the terrible words, "I never knew you," and find ourselves, as C. S. Lewis put it, "banished from the presence of Him who is present everywhere and erased from the knowledge of Him who knows all." (pp. 14–15)

What we think just isn't important. But what God thinks is. And this caution should drive us even closer to the pages of Scripture to understand how popular concepts of spirituality are changing and how we can use them to the advantage of the church.

A NEW WAY OF EATING

What do you know about the Jewish Passover meal? Just before their hasty departure from Egypt, God instructed the children of Israel to eat a meal that symbolized how He would deal with them on their journey and throughout their history. And as the angel of death touched each household that night, they would have vivid memories that their houses were "passed over." A year into their journey into the wilderness, about the time when they might forget God's goodness, they were to repeat this Passover meal as a reminder of God's goodness.

Centuries later, God sent His Son to introduce a "new covenant" of love and forgiveness—again, a reminder that God was "passing over" their former sins. "All have sinned and fall short of the glory of God; they are now justified by His grace as a gift, through the redemption that is in Christ Jesus, whom God put forward as a sacrifice of atonement by His blood, effective through faith. He did this to show His righteousness, because in His divine forbearance He had passed over the sins previously committed" (Romans 3:23–25 NRSV).

What does this new covenant mean to you? Can you see the value in God asking His people to repeat this meal throughout their journey—not just in the wilderness of Sinai, but throughout their journey through the wilderness called life? What is the value of repeating the "new" Passover meal—the Lord's Supper?

Throughout their journey, God took opportunities to remind His people of His grace and their helplessness. When they encountered opposition, God would ask them, "Who are you and where do you come from?" (Joshua 9:8b). And then they would have to recite their history, which included the first Passover. Don't you think they would have realized how miraculous and important God's presence was to them? Sometimes they did, and sometimes they didn't. How about you? When do you realize and when do you forget?

TIME TRAVELER

A man sat by the side of the road holding a sign that read "Stranded time traveler. Parts broken. Need help!" What do you think about this scenario? How would you respond?

Do you ever feel like a stranded time traveler? The world has changed so much that perhaps you feel like you belong in another time. When do you feel most "stranded"? In which time would you most prefer to live? Having dealt with so much change in the present, how will you deal with the future?

In his vision of the future, John saw God living directly with His people. "What would that be like?" you wonder. Just like going across town to see your friends? What if you could visit God anytime you wished? This is what John saw, and this is what we can experience as we rejoice in the newness of Christ:

> Then I saw a new heaven and a new earth, for the first heaven and the first earth had passed away, and there was no longer any sea. I saw the Holy City, the new Jerusalem, coming down out of heaven from God, prepared as a bride beautifully dressed for her husband. And I heard a loud voice from the throne saying, "Now the dwelling of God is with men, and He will live with them. They will be His people, and God Himself will be with them and be their God. He will wipe every tear from their eyes. There will be no more death or mourning or crying or pain, for the old order of things has passed away." He who was seated on the throne said, "I am making everything new!" Then He said, "Write this down, for these words are trustworthy and true." He said to me: "It is done. I am the Alpha and the Omega, the Beginning and the End. To him who is thirsty I will give to drink without cost from the spring of the water of life. He who overcomes will inherit all this, and I will be his God and he will be My son." (Revelation 21:1–7)

Religion and the forms of the church may be changing. But the God of the new covenant is the same as the God of the old covenant. God is the same today, and He will be the same tomorrow. What a wonderful change we can expect when He returns to take us home!

FOR DISCUSSION

1. Discuss ways in which you and your church have changed your way of spreading Christ's message.
2. Refer to the chart that compared modern and postmodern characteristics. Do these changes in perception suggest anything about the way

you plan your worship or other church activities? Do you think the leadership of your church considers these factors when they plan church-wide activities? Do you think they should?

3. If, as researchers and social scientists have suggested, people today are more likely to examine sources of authority other than the Bible, how are Christians to approach outreach and evangelism? In what ways will worship and social gatherings be different? In what new ways can we apply the Holy Scriptures?

4. How much can you change before you change too much? Do you think that people can become so excited about change and improvement that they lose sight of the changeless Christ? What would you do if that happened in your church?

5. What are we waiting for? What excuses have you used to put off witnessing? How will your understanding of the modern and postmodern eras help you overcome these obstacles?

6. How does the following Bible verse relate to what you have learned about the postmodern era? "Praise be to the God and Father of our Lord Jesus Christ! In His great mercy He has given us new birth into a living hope through the resurrection of Jesus Christ from the dead" (1 Peter 1:3).

4

THE CHANGING
AND GROWING CHURCH

CHANGE IS ALL AROUND US

A man gave his son a couple of dollars and sent him down to the corner store for some milk. Soon the son was back and said, "That store isn't there anymore, Dad. There's an oil-change place there now!" The father was surprised but accepted the remark without further question. It wasn't until the next day as he drove to work that he realized his son had walked in the wrong direction! The corner store was still where it always was, but a new oil-change place had sprung up on an empty lot a block in the other direction. The father had simply accepted change without question.

Alvin Toffler, in his now-classic book *Future Shock*, chronicles the rapid changes of the 1960s and 1970s and talks about the shock of bumping into a future for which we are often unprepared. Toffler suggests that the only constant thing is change. People have been conditioned to accept change. For some that is scary; for others it is accepted without question.

When Jesus lived on earth, many changes took place too. The Romans occupied the land and threatened to take away personal and corporate freedoms. Greek became a universal language which, in turn, promoted international travel and commerce. More and better roads made travel easier.

The idea of a Messiah, however, was nothing new. According to one of Judaism's own leaders, Gamaliel, many so-called messiahs had arisen, gathered a following, and quickly vanished into the desert (Acts 5:36–37). But, as Gamaliel cautioned his people, "Therefore, in the present case I advise you: Leave these men alone! Let them go! For if their purpose or activity is of human origin, it will fail. But if it is from God, you will not be able to stop these men; you will only find yourselves fighting against God" (Acts 5:38–39). As we look at and perhaps critique the changing and growing church of today, we must be careful not to oppose that which God has not opposed.

It is God who has charged us to spread His Good News, and He has promised the success of His Word. Shortly before Jesus ascended into heaven, He said, "All authority in heaven and on earth has been given to Me. Therefore go and make disciples of all nations, baptizing them in the name of the Father and of the Son and of the Holy Spirit, and teaching them to obey everything I have commanded you. And surely I am with you always, to the very end of the age" (Matthew 28:18–20).

We are to share God's Word with everyone. But not everyone can hear or see it, so we must seek ways to spread the Word most effectively in every time and at every place. We can be certain, however, that God's Word will succeed in reaching people (Isaiah 55:11).

The form of the church has changed through the years, but it remains the visible representation of Christ's kingdom on earth, a gathering of humans marching under Christ's orders and directed to do His will. The first Christians were Jews. They struggled over the issue of circumcision (Acts 15). As the church grew numerically, they had to deal with the issue of individual property. Apparently, the early Christians trusted each other with such great intensity that they kept their wealth and property in common, distributing it to whomever had a need (Acts 2:44–45). But as Satan and sin worked their way, some people began to hold back and the system began breaking down (Ananias and Sapphira, Acts 5). The church changed again.

Some "churches" met in the homes of members. Some met

at the synagogue, where believers of "the Way" had previously gathered as Jews. Sometimes they simply met at a well or by a river—wherever people gathered out of need, necessity, or habit. It seems clear that Jesus Himself wasn't as concerned about form and style as He was about substance. He remarked, "Heaven and earth will pass away, but My words will never pass away" (Matthew 24:35).

As we examine the modern-day church, we discover that it is changing and growing. Since God has charged us to "grow" His church, we have the responsibility of dealing with the changes we encounter or initiate and safeguarding against changes that He would forbid.

WHERE IS THE CHURCH HEADED?

Following a series of serious earthquakes, a waiter in a Los Angeles restaurant said, "I can't take it anymore. My kids can't take it anymore. We're going back to Kansas. No place out here is safe from quakes" (Sweet, *FaithQuakes*, p. 7). Not just in the church, but throughout our society and even our world, many people say the same of the changes they see and experience: "I can't take it anymore. I want to go back!" Which changes would you reverse if you could?

Leonard Sweet, in his book *FaithQuakes*, says, "The church is now living in one of the biggest social earthquakes in history—the post-modern reality rift" (p. 8). What are some of the tremors that you feel in culture, society, and the church? Individual congregations as well as entire church bodies must examine the social earthquakes and decide if they must flee to safety or stay and cope with the situation. They must ask what Christ would do to make the church grow both in numbers and in faith. And they will find the answers in the most likely place: God's Word.

One phenomenon of response to changing lifestyles is the church growth movement. Some well-intentioned Christians have cautioned against this movement. Some warn against the variety of worship aimed at entertainment rather than worship of the true and living God. Some churches have "seeker" services, aimed at attracting the unchurched. Others insist that the church "should be more concerned about meeting the needs of the unchurched person than meeting the needs of people who already believe in Jesus Christ and support the church with their faithful and regular involvement and monies" (Ernie V. Lassman, "Church Growth and Worship," *Concordia Theological Quarterly* 62, no. 1 [1998], 39–62).

Congregations will find easy access to proponents of the church growth movement, some of whom will offer consultation services for a fee. However, congregations must always examine such services in light of both Scripture and their mission statement.

WINDOWS INTO THE TWENTY-FIRST CENTURY

An interesting phenomenon of the last years of the twentieth century is an organization called Leadership Network. Bob Buford, a television executive from Texas, disseminates information to church leaders throughout the country. Although Leadership Network is not really a church, in many ways it acts like one. It teaches, leads, and shares the Good News of Jesus Christ with people. It also shares the "latest ideas" with Christians throughout the world. One fascinating way Leadership Network shares its idea is through a monthly "Net Fax," which is sent free to church offices through a facsimile machine.

One recent "Net Fax" listed "Five Windows into the 21st Century Church":

1. **Effective leadership** in the church is moving from a single leader to a team, from a focus on preaching and pastoral care to one proactive in leadership vision and mission. To be effective, leadership in the local church must be decentralized, as the pastor(s) and staff become equippers of

others. Many churches are heavily involved in creating mission and vision statements. These will be used in many ways.

2. **Lay mobilization** encompasses two well-known and strongly biblical concepts: the priesthood of all believers (1 Peter 2:9) and the variety of spiritual gifts given to each individual to be used in serving the whole body. Leadership is involved in a systematic approach to identify and encourage individuals within the church to utilize their blessings to build the church.

3. **Cultural connectedness** recognizes that we are in a global society with the largest population centers in multicultural urban areas. The church cannot ignore these conditions and must understand and engage the entire culture if it is to be a significant force in preparing Christians to meet the future.

4. **Authentic community** recognizes that the church, especially in the twenty-first century, will be driven by people's needs rather than by a desire to perpetuate a particular program or institutional church. Small groups are often formed for the purposes of caring, learning, support, ministry, and accountability. This practice is popularly called the "meta" church. These groups place strong emphasis on disciple-making, worship, prayer, and a sense of something that in the biblical narrative would be called a journey but in modern times is often looked upon as a "holy adventure."

5. **Kingdom collaboration** is an openness to partnerships and networks with other Christians and organizations. These groups often cross denominational lines.

We must be cautious against simply reducing the church to its lowest common denominator when it comes to maintaining pure biblical doctrine. But we can also learn much from others and their church organizations.

As churches journey through the waning years of the twentieth century, they must constantly remind themselves that an arbitrary date divides the twentieth and twenty-first centuries.

But many changes and movements in the church are not arbitrary or coincidental.

We have looked at changes that have taken place in Christian churches and that are likely to occur within the lives of Christians in the near future. We can look back and learn much from history. But we must also be discerning students of what the future is to bring. We do not know exactly what the future holds, but God has given us interesting and insightful windows through which to wonder.

MAJOR CHANGES CLOUD HINDSIGHT

Several major changes in the world prevent us from accurately seeing the past. One is the "fall into sin," as recorded in Genesis 3. Another is the great flood, recorded in Genesis 6. In more recent times, the Protestant Reformation, the Industrial Revolution, and the several major world wars prevent us from accurately seeing what the world was like many years ago. But we can study how earlier church leaders dealt with problems and seek to understand what God says to us through the events of history.

Consider the origin of sin and its massive effect on the world. Paul describes it this way:

> Therefore, just as sin entered the world through one man, and death through sin, and in this way death came to all men, because all sinned—for before the law was given, sin was in the world. But sin is not taken into account when there is no law. Nevertheless, death reigned from the time of Adam to the time of Moses, even over those who did not sin by breaking a command, as did Adam, who was a pattern of the one to come. (Romans 5:12–14)

Sin prevents us from clearly seeing our past, but God's grace allows us to know that we are forgiven and acceptable to God! Scripture says that before the fall, God "walk[ed] in the garden in the cool of the day" (Genesis 3:8). On days when we wish we could have that kind of close fellowship with God, we must read Scripture, remember our personal history, and trust the Holy Spirit to give us a growing future relationship with God.

The Protestant Reformation changed the way the world looked at religion and spirituality. As the result of the Reformation, God's Word became widely distributed in the language of the common people. The invention of a printing press with moveable type allowed rapid and widespread dissemination of Scripture and ideas about spirituality.

Until the Gospel was preached and printed in its pure form, people feared God. They sought shelter in monasteries and convents where they felt safe from the evil influences of the outside world and could perform some good that God might consider acceptable. What was the world like when people thought they could buy forgiveness and eternal life? It must have been a dark, sin-filled world. What kind of hope did those people experience?

We live in an age of what is often called a "quick-fix mentality." No wonder that Paul, in Romans 1, talks about people exchanging the truth about God for a lie:

> For although they knew God, they neither glorified Him as God nor gave thanks to Him, but their thinking became futile and their foolish hearts were darkened. Although they claimed to be wise, they became fools and exchanged the glory of the immortal God for images made to look like mortal man and birds and animals and reptiles. Therefore God gave them over in the sinful desires of their hearts to sexual impurity for the degrading of their bodies with one another. They exchanged the truth of God for a lie, and worshiped and served created things rather than the Creator—who is forever praised. Amen. (Romans 1:21–25)

What an apt description of idolatry! Worshiping the created rather than the Creator! This description fit God's people in Paul's time. What examples show that it fits God's people in the present time also?

Another major change in our world that also impacts the church and Christians is the "information explosion." Business and personal computers, online services, and the resulting instant networking of our world have changed the way most organizations and many individuals go about their daily activities.

A recent news article indicates the immensity and far-reaching implications of this questionable wonder: a computer software glitch coupling stationary communications satellites caused banks, ATMs, and gasoline pumps to stop taking credit and debit cards for a couple of days. The headline on the news article stated, "Welcome to a preview of the Millennium!" What many people fear will happen at midnight on December 31, 1999, was brought much closer. We realize just how dependent upon computers and instant information we have become. Where once the total information available in print was doubling every 50 or 25 years, currently it doubles every 6 years, and the interval is decreasing steadily.

All this change, and yet we still have Ecclesiastes 3! Solomon says there is nothing new under the sun. Yet we certainly scramble to gain possessions and to know more facts. But God has made it clear that information—even lots of it—is not a substitute for faith in Him and relationships with other people.

If spiritual, cultural, and political upheavals create barriers to viewing the past, what about the future? What will the twenty-first century be like? How will we maintain a clear spiritual outlook that centers on Jesus Christ? We certainly can't look into the future—God has reserved that for Himself. But He has told us certain things about the future—especially about the relationship between God and ourselves. "I write these things to you who believe in the name of the Son of God so that you may know that you have eternal life" (1 John 5:13). With faith in Christ, we know for sure that we have eternal life. In fact, since our first call by God in Baptism, we are certain that we are living in eternal life—right here and now! And we can celebrate that close relationship to God each day of our existence.

THE SHAPE OF THE CHURCH

What differences do you notice in church architecture? Some churches are long and narrow—some are almost circular. The long, narrow churches, often built toward the end of the last century and the beginning half of this century, were often modeled after the huge cathedrals of Europe. Many are patterned after the earliest Christian churches—in the shape of a cross. What a wonderful witness to the Savior! And what a wonderful and functional shape! However, as churches became larger and people sought to participate more in worship services, architects "broke the mold," so to speak. They devised ways to bring people closer to the "front" and the worship leaders. Churches were built "in the round." Everyone could be close enough to hear. And everyone could be close enough to see. (These obstacles are also overcome with amplification systems and with video equipment and huge screens.)

Another development is that some churches are interested in creating multi-use space and no longer permanently attach pews or benches to the floor. This creates space that is useful at times other than Sunday morning and for uses other than large group worship experiences.

ORGANIZATIONAL SHAPES

What is the organizational shape of your church? Do you have a church council, a voters' group, and officers that are elected every year or two? Do you often have difficulty locating enough volunteers to staff a good slate of officers?

Consider how the organizational shape of the church has changed over the years. In the Middle Ages, the pastor of a European church was easily the most educated and respected person in the church and community. Sometimes, although this was not the intent, church leadership positions were sold in order to raise funds rather than voted on by the church leadership or congregations, as is most often the case today.

The church degenerated to the extent that not only positions in the church were sold and traded, but forgiveness was sold as well. When the young Martin Luther arrived to serve as pastor at a parish church, he discovered that many people no longer attended worship because they were crossing the river to buy letters of "indulgence" from a man who actually represented the leader of the church, the pope.

When Luther posted his famous Ninety-Five Theses on the door of the Castle Church in Wittenberg, Germany, he was largely reacting against these abuses and not against the whole church itself. In fact, when a so-called "counterrevolution" threatened all churches in his area, Luther protested vigorously. He had not wanted to throw everything out, but only to dismiss that which disagreed with Scripture.

"Clericalism" became prevalent. Under this system, the pastor was the unquestioned leader of the church and, in many cases, the community. Luther was appalled when, shortly after his installation as a pastor, he visited other pastors and learned that many were uneducated, had no idea what the Bible taught, and functioned more like political leaders and bankers. Perhaps this is why some people suspect the church's relationship to money today!

Many churches in our country operate with what is known as a "congregational" structure. Patterned after the democracy upon which the United States was founded, leaders, both lay and professional, are elected either by representatives of the group or by the whole congregation itself. Individual congregations are generally viewed as autonomous, but they may work together to train pastors and other professional church workers, conduct mission work, and provide other services.

Some organizations, such as the Roman Catholic and Orthodox churches, still operate in the "episcopal" form of church government where religious leaders make decisions from the top down with little congregational autonomy.

As previously mentioned, one modern movement, called the "small group" or "meta" church, recognizes that as churches grow larger, people who seek close personal relationships want something that can be found only in smaller groups. Rather than break up the larger churches, which offer important benefits such as teaching and sending stations, smaller groups within the church form around specific interests and tasks to be performed. Patterned after Christ's Great Commission in Matthew 28, these small groups are geared for growth and expansion.

Most organizations experience conflict as various factions promote or resist change. Tension and struggle are natural elements of any organization. Consider one organizational struggle that the church experienced long ago. Recall that Jesus was a Jew and His first followers were Jews from Galilee. He called them away from other vocations. Some were in positions of questionable integrity. Their seminary training was "on the go," as Jesus went about teaching, healing, and calling people to repent. Unlike most religious organizers before Him, Jesus did not baptize anyone. He built no buildings, and He didn't establish formal rules or guidelines for organization. Instead, He went about doing good and loving people. He taught people in simple terms, like His summaries of the two tables of the Ten Commandments: "Love the Lord your God with all your heart and with all your soul and with all your mind and with all your strength. ... Love your neighbor as yourself. There is no commandment greater than these" (Mark 12:30–31).

It was natural that the very first Christians were Jews. But God sent Gentile outsiders into their midst. Then God performed a marvelous feat that showed just how great He really is. For raw material He took a notorious unbeliever named Saul of Tarsus. Saul was highly educated and advanced in the Jewish religion and the political interests of the Pharisees. The high point of Saul's career had been the arrests and convictions he made when he apprehended followers of Christ and led them to trial and possible execution.

Do you think it was a coincidence that God caught Saul just

at the high point of his career, knocked him off his horse, and changed his life radically? God made an undeniable impression on Saul that he proclaimed over and over again. "I am not ashamed of the gospel, because it is the power of God for the salvation of everyone who believes: first for the Jew, then for the Gentile" (Romans 1:16).

Saul changed his name to Paul, probably to emphasize the dramatic change that God had worked in his life. God then specifically sent Paul to share His Word with the Gentiles whom the Jews considered outsiders. They wanted nothing to do with Gentiles, but God was introducing them to a huge change. He was teaching them something new.

Acts 15 reports another conflict in the early church. Some leaders of the church in Antioch demanded that new converts be circumcised, as all Jews had been when they first became "religious." But the apostle Paul and his friend Barnabas, who had been out sharing the Gospel with Gentiles, sharply disagreed with them.

When the missionary pair shared how successful they had been in sharing the Gospel with Gentiles, some felt that no further hindrance should be placed on their conversion. Peter, the leader of the Jerusalem church, spoke the loudest in favor of this plan. But the visiting church leaders insisted that Gentiles ought to be in some way obedient to the Jewish laws. Another leader of the church, James, quoted the prophet Amos. He reminded the other leaders that although God did lift up the Jews, He also promised room in His kingdom for Gentiles who responded to His Word. James suggested that a letter be distributed to the Gentile churches: circumcision was not specifically required by this letter, but four other stipulations were laid down for Gentile Christians, probably identifying behaviors that particularly repulsed the Jews (Acts 15:20).

The point here is that church leaders met and made a decision, based partly on the tremendous response they had witnessed as the Gospel was preached to the Gentiles and partly on what God had said through Moses. They averted a potential split and preserved peace. It is also important to note that when the letter was distributed, church leaders and Gentiles were pleased with the outcome (Acts 15:31). They had effectively confronted change in a manner that pleased both God and people.

In our times, there are similar controversies that threaten to undermine the unity we have in Christ. Some wish that all churches would have a uniform worship style and structure. Others look at changing culture and welcome it as long as the Gospel is not changed. Some concentrate on sin and condemn it. Others embrace sinners who repent and invite them to return to Christ. These issues will not go away. The church will continue to be in conflict as long as it exists on earth. We must be willing to seek God's will as we confront differences and be willing to hold fast to the truth of God's Word.

Do You Have Change for a Paradigm?

Do you have a long-term relationship with an organized and traditional church, either personally or through your family? Can you imagine the church of 50 years ago sponsoring a small group designed to help people who have gone through a divorce or who are struggling because they are single parents? What about a group to support those who abuse alcohol or drugs? (Years ago you couldn't even say the words "alcohol," "divorce," or "unwed mothers"!)

Today, churches seek to attract those who are hurting. Christian churches sponsor small groups designed to give direction and support to those who struggle with the backlash and effects of sin in their lives. We no longer seek to label, mark, and judge people. We wish to reach them with the Gospel of Christ's forgiveness. Many modern congregations also maintain church Web pages and invite people to meetings and other events. Some churches support free health care and counseling centers.

As the future rushes toward (and sometimes past) us, we cannot bury our heads in the sand and ignore the changes around us. We may not like all the changes we see, but can we stop them? When and why would we want to?

THE CHURCH SHALL NEVER PERISH

Consider the language, style of worship, and type of music used in worship today. Those born in the so-called postmodern decades prefer different styles than many churches offer. Must we require them to sit through worship that doesn't reflect their mode of expression? One person's greatest spiritual experience may be sitting alone in silence, another's may be listening to a loud organ, while still another person may prefer an electric guitar. Within the truth of the Gospel there are certain freedoms that God allows. Some fear that a variety of worship styles within a particular congregation will divide the congregation. Others fear that the congregation is already divided. Those who feel uncomfortable in what is termed "traditional" worship just don't come, or they go where a style of worship matches their preferences.

Will the organized church perish? Probably not in the reader's lifetime. But its traditions will change over time, and God willing, that's not all bad. Consider the earliest Christians. What would they think of our church?

FOR DISCUSSION

1. Author Leonard Sweet observes, "In one poll of mall shoppers, only 25 percent said they came to buy something specific. Three-quarters of them came just to gaze and get their 'eyeball' kicks" (*FaithQuakes*, p. 23). What does this suggest about the way Christ would have His church proceed within the world at this very moment?
2. In your opinion, how is the church growth movement headed in the right direction? Do you agree with criticism of the movement? How does this criticism agree or disagree with Christ's Great Commission from

Matthew 28? As we begin the twenty-first century, how do you believe Christians can chart a middle course that is faithful to God and to our traditions?

3. Examine materials distributed by your church or other local groups. Check out schedules as printed in public media. What kinds of groups do churches sponsor that didn't even exist 10 or 20 years ago?

4. Which of the following would you endorse for your church? Which would you not endorse? Why?
   - Seminary training of clergy is optional.
   - Worship is contemporary in style.
   - Lay leadership is highly valued and encouraged.
   - Extensive small group ministries are formed.
   - Clergy and worshipers usually dress informally.
   - Tolerance of different personal styles is respected.
   - Pastors tend to be understated, humble, and self-revealing.
   - Gifts of the Holy Spirit are identified and affirmed.
   - Bible-centered teaching predominates over topical sermonizing.

5. Is the church becoming too much like a business? Is the church catering to the lowest common denominator? Review the Scriptures touched on in this chapter. What is God saying to you?

6. In an era when all churches are facing changes and many are experiencing unexpectedly rapid growth, how will you respond when you "do church"? What does it mean to be a Christian, and how can you be sure you are faithful to the Christ who founded your church?

5

SPIRITUALITY: FROM MOUNTAINTOP TO CYBERCHURCH!

TO THE ENDS OF THE EARTH

After His suffering, He [Jesus] showed Himself to these men and gave many convincing proofs that He was alive. He appeared to them over a period of forty days and spoke about the kingdom of God. On one occasion, while He was eating with them, He gave them this command: "Do not leave Jerusalem, but wait for the gift My Father promised, which you have heard Me speak about. For John baptized with water, but in a few days you will be baptized with the Holy Spirit." So when they met together, they asked Him, "Lord, are You at this time going to restore the kingdom to Israel?" He said to them: "It is not for you to know the times or dates the Father has set by His own authority. But you will receive power when the Holy Spirit comes on you; and you will be My witnesses in Jerusalem, and in all Judea and Samaria, and to the ends of the earth." (Acts 1:3–8)

In the first part of Jesus' instructions to His followers, He encouraged them to stay in Jerusalem. But then He directed them outward. He wanted them to look for others they could reach with the wonderful message of God's presence. He suggested that eventually they would go to the ends of the earth.

Earlier, when the disciples asked Jesus for signs of His coming, He said that many of the signs had already come: wars, rumors of wars, unrest among nations. "And this gospel of the kingdom will be preached in the whole world as a testimony to all nations, and then the end will come" (Matthew 24:14).

Considering the advent of radio, television, computers,

satellites, and the Internet, is it possible to reach every person in the world with the Gospel of Jesus Christ? Many churches pioneered the use of radio in the 1930s and television in the 1950s to spread the Gospel. Is it possible that the broad popularity of the Internet will help to accomplish global evangelism?

Consider what you now know about spirituality. There are many advocates of spirituality in the world today. Some are of God, and some are not. Some promote the help of a supreme being outside yourself, and some encourage people to recognize the divine within themselves. The New Age movement unashamedly says, "You are god! You can do anything." Where do you think churches and religion are headed?

Some religious and spiritual organizations have identified a profile of spiritually receptive young adults and specifically plan ways to reach them. Can Christian churches learn anything from these strategies?

One church identified as its target individuals who were well- educated, were conscious of health and fitness, preferred large rather than small groups, were skeptical of organized religion, liked contemporary music, preferred the casual and informal over the formal, and were generally overextended in both time and money. Thinking back to biblical reports, we might see Jesus, the disciples, and the early church leaders picking targets for their message too. Think about their various audiences. What was different in the way they approached Jews and Gentiles, Pharisees and common people?

YOU'LL NEVER MISS

Some people consider the evangelistic efforts of their churches to be like Charlie Brown, of "Peanuts" cartoon fame, practicing archery. Instead of shooting at the target, he aims at a fence and then walks over and draws a target around the arrow as it sticks in the wood. Lucy walks up and says, "Why are you doing that, Charlie Brown?"

He replies, "This way I never miss!"

Churches whose evangelism efforts consist of shooting and then seeing what they have hit miss the intentionality with which God charged His people in Acts 1. Granted, He told them to go to the ends of the earth, but they were to start where they were—in Jerusalem. Then they were to move to the Judean countryside. Although they probably weren't too eager about the instruction, Jesus also directed them north to Samaria—to a land of racially mixed and nearly "untouchable" people. Finally, God sent this little group of Jews "to the ends of the earth." According to some nonbiblical literature, scholars have identified "the ends of the earth" as Rome, which is also the location of the apostle Paul's final journey and the end of history recorded in the New Testament.

It is clear that God wants His people to spread the Gospel. And it is clear that He wants them to share His Good News in many and various locations.

Different people have different targets—different audiences. Jesus said, "I was sent only to the lost sheep of Israel" (Matthew 15:24). Yet when a Gentile woman approached Him, begging to take the crumbs that fell from His table, Jesus didn't turn her away (Matthew 15:27).

You will recall that Peter and Paul were sent to preach God's Good News to different audiences. Paul said he had been entrusted with the task of preaching the Gospel to the Gentiles, just as Peter had been sent to the Jews.

Once, many churches were content to simply target those living nearby, with occasional foreign missionary emphases and interests. But today, people nearby often consider their home to be their castle—complete with impenetrable walls. People value their privacy. They can be as difficult to reach as tribes residing in remote nations.

The church must be intentional and deliberate about reaching out with the Gospel. It must overcome obstacles. Two decades ago, urban congregations talked about helping members relocate in high-rise security apartments so as to gain an "in." Now churches are asking where they can we get the next foot in the door to reach the unreachable.

Are you surprised to know that the fastest growing segment of the currently unchurched population are those from 15 to 30 years old? Sociologists call them "Gen Xers." This group has more money and free time than any other group, but they also discriminate more in spending their money and time. They have grown up in the era of fast food and quick fix. There is a revival of interest in spirituality among the Gen Xers, but many are unlikely to set foot in an institutional church. As unlikely as they are to participate in institutionalized religion, it's equally likely that they use computers at home and on the job. Therefore, the Internet may be one of many outreach strategies churches can use to spread God's message of salvation.

CHRISTIANITY ONLINE

A number of churches are starting so-called "Gen X services" at a variety of times in order to attract the young and spiritual but uncommitted. A recent survey by the Barna Research Group of Oxnard, California, discovered that a growing number of Gen X individuals are using the Internet for spiritual discovery and religious discussion. Barna's random questioning of 620 13- to 18-year-olds in September 1997 and 1,006 adults in January 1998 showed that by the year 2010, 10 to 20 percent of the U.S. population is likely to rely on the Internet for their primary or exclusive source of religious and spiritual information. Sixteen percent of teens said they currently use the Internet exclusively as a substitute for church, and 12 percent of adults already use the Internet for faith matters.

The Barna Group drew the following conclusion from their findings:

> A large portion of teenagers use the Net for conversation with others. A substantial number of cyberchatters engage in dialogue

related to faith, spirituality, religion, meaning, and truth—the types of conversations that are often initiated or fostered by churches. Teens do not think of those conversations as religious expression, but the sense of community and spiritual beliefs fostered by such dialogue on spiritual matters is identical to what the traditional church seeks to create within its congregations. ("Is the Sun Rising on 'Cyberchurch'? And Will Your Teens 'Attend' It?" *Reporter*, May 1998, p. 15)

In a recent listing of pastors and churches in southern Minnesota, about 55 percent of them included e-mail addresses. At a voters' meeting in one large congregation in Minneapolis, 125 people were in attendance when a proposed Web page for the church was discussed. Someone, who by admission knew nothing about the Internet or Web pages, questioned spending church money on something he felt would not touch many lives. Someone else asked for a show of hands as to how many people had e-mail addresses and regularly used the Internet. Over 60 percent of the people raised their hands. The motion passed without further discussion. This Web page will allow members and visitors to access basic information about the church, its staff, and current and future activities. College students and travelers will be able to keep current with church activities by accessing the Web page from remote locations.

Using this technology elsewhere, one youth pastor regularly communicates with college students in distant cities. He provides a weekly devotion just for them and keeps them abreast of any developments back on the home front, including Sunday morning youth "alumni" brunches during holidays when these students are likely to be back in town. Another pastor provides weekly devotions, shares prayer concerns, and offers brief news items on a weekly e-mail publication. It takes him about 30 minutes to create the e-mail and 30 seconds to send. Can you think of any other ways to use the Internet and the World Wide Web?

Pentecost Online

Just before Jesus ascended into heaven, He gathered His disciples on a hill outside of Jerusalem and tried to prepare them for what was about to happen. But like little children being told that their parents are going on a long vacation, the disciples couldn't fathom exactly what it would be like without Him. And we can't imagine the future either. Remember Alvin Toffler's book *Future Shock*? He talked about the massive changes we were encountering—and that book was written 30 years ago.

In 1982, John Naisbitt wrote another important futurist book entitled *Megatrends: Ten Dimensions for Transforming Our Lives*. It was an instant success. People wanted to learn how to deal with the future because it was coming at them faster and faster. Then in 1990, Naisbitt, together with Patricia Abundene, caught up to "the future" by writing *Megatrends 2000: Ten New Directions for the 1990s*.

As mentioned in an earlier chapter, the rate at which global information doubles is accelerating at a frightening pace. Technology maintains a similar velocity. Today, even the smallest home computers are more powerful than the biggest business or industrial computers of two decades ago. The computers that control many functions in most automobiles are faster and more sophisticated than those used in college by the engineers who designed them.

How will the church and religious organizations of the future use computers, the Internet, and e-mail? "Net Fax," a faxed monthly newsletter put out by the Leadership Network in Dallas, Texas, has suggested the following possibilities. Consider which ones you might find useful, and inquire whether your church is already using technology in this way.

1. **Evangelism and outreach**—A church Web site could include 20 FAQs (Web shorthand for "Frequently Asked Questions") about Christianity. Some congregations include information that allows users to search for informa-

tion on Bible study opportunities and to access biblical resources. Some even include short stories or testimonials of faith and include a "button" that the reader can "click" with a mouse to initiate personal contact.

2. **Communication, both internal and external**—Church Web pages often include information for "outsiders" and potential visitors, including a schedule of activities, maps and directions for coming to the church, and names of people they might e-mail or phone for further personal information. ("High tech requires high touch" is an important motto to remember!)

   Like many offices, some churches use the Internet and e-mail to communicate within the organization. Consider the convenience of simply typing a message and sending it to one or several members of a church. You don't have to walk to the office mailbox, and there are no papers to lose. One person can communicate with a hundred people just as easily as a dozen staff members can. And it's nearly instantaneous!

   What if the members of a board, committee, or small-group Bible study could send agendas, meeting minutes, simple greetings, or prayer requests without leaving their home or office? While it is still important to make personal contact, many advocates of the cyberchurch have suggested that electronic communication actually draws people closer together more quickly and creates a tighter and stronger community.

3. **Distance learning**—What if members of a Sunday school or Bible class could get notes or assignments even when they were absent or ill? Sermons could be transmitted to shut-ins. Technology experts tell us that it is possible to instantly transmit audio and video messages from your church to others via the Internet. Can you think of any other possibilities?

4. **Resource Center**—As suggested in number 1 above, a church or religious organization could become a resource

center for Bible and other research information. One denomination published a costly and bulky book in which they included statistics about congregations throughout the country. This information is now available more quickly and economically on a Web page. It is available at the click of a button, or it can be "downloaded" and printed!

When Jesus promised the Pentecost explosion of languages that occurred when the Holy Spirit fell on His disciples, do you think they anticipated how much their lives would change? Can you say the same of the impact of technology, especially computers and the Internet, on our lives? We must be careful not to worship computers and technology. But we can use these wonderful gifts of God to enhance our spiritual lives. And we can use the Internet to spread the Gospel too.

All this is not to say that communications technology will put missionaries, both domestic and foreign, on the unemployment line. As powerful and broad a tool as communication technology is, perhaps it helps us to keep our perspective when we realize that only 1 percent of the world's population has used the Internet; 75 percent have never used a telephone; and 70 percent cannot read (from the Armed Forces supplement to the *Lutheran Witness*, August 1998).

HIGH TECH AND HIGH TOUCH

People who are active on the Internet and the Web may never meet those with whom they communicate. They can "talk" to others as frequently or infrequently as they choose. Unlike a telephone that begs to be answered, electronic mail can be ignored or even deleted sight unseen. This is why human-resources professionals in the business domain coined the phrase "High tech requires high touch!" Those who do their business in isolation, or even at home, still need human interaction. Most computers have a "help" button, which users can "click" to access a database of helpful information when they have problems. But will isolated individuals seek personal help, especially with their interpersonal relationships?

For those who seem to thrive online, churches and spiritual groups must pay special attention to the interpersonal needs that remain. Those who have experienced frequent broken relationships may deliberately isolate themselves in the relative "privacy" of their computers. Christians must be sensitive to their wishes at the same time as they discern interpersonal needs.

Perhaps the future of the cyberchurch is yet another way to learn how to share our spiritual journey with others. Many who have been hurt can proceed just as far and as fast as they want. And they can do so without being personally exposed to danger or more hurt.

Computers invite a technological form of interaction. By comparison, television, one of the biggest technological advances of the 1940s and 1950s, contributed to a passive generation of people often called "couch potatoes." Computers have changed that situation. There is now "interaction" with the screen. And with that interaction, many possibilities have opened up for Christ's people. The church is no longer defined by the past. It is also defined and shaped by how we perceive the future.

Methods of communication change faster than people change. In the future, churches and religious groups must make special provisions to provide personal care for individuals, especially when they ask for it. They will also need to avoid any pretense of exclusiveness based on technological experience or hardware required for communication. An older technology, the telephone "help line," can help too. Some churches have made available the telephone number of a staff member or counselor who is "on call" at various times during the week. Many provide "dial-a-devotion" and telephone-accessible "prayer chains."

There is one thing of which we can be certain: God is in our future. Jesus promised to be with us to the end of the world (Matthew 28:20). May we take that promise to our hearts and those of others—online and up front!

WHAT IS TO PREVENT ME FROM BEING BAPTIZED?

Perhaps it has already happened. Just imagine this powerful scenario. Two people are chatting on the computer. The first person, José, a young man, has recently lost his job and just needs someone to talk to. He is in school and things aren't going well. He is alienated from his parents and wouldn't think of talking to them about his problems. The second person, Art, is a retired engineer, recently widowed, who simply hacks away on his computer for a few hours each evening. They have become acquainted, seemingly at random, across nearly a thousand miles in the midwestern United States. They have exchanged hopes and dreams. When the conversation finally comes around to religion, the engineer haltingly begins to share. He is a lifelong Christian, knowledgeable about the Bible, but somewhat hesitant in sharing his faith. The young man has had no contact with an organized church, but he is searching. He is asking spiritual, not religious, questions. He types to the engineer,

José: How can you believe in a God who allowed your wife to die such a horrible death with cancer?

Art: I don't know, José. I guess I just believe. A lot of it is like blind faith. I believe that God created this world—even though I've never seen Him. I believe He loves me, even though at times it doesn't seem like it. Just like my kids didn't always think I loved them.

José: Yeah. I can relate to that. My folks are always ragging on me about school, grades, and money. That's why I'm living way out here, away from them—and not back at home. I'd really like to be there and save money.

Art: So, José. Just what do you believe about God?

José: I don't know. I just have a hard time believing in a God who allows all kinds of bad things to happen. Like your wife. And my job. Excuse me, Art. I didn't mean to compare them—yours is much worse.

Art: No, I understand. And that's exactly what I'm getting at. God is a God of everyone and every situation. Sometimes we pray to God and try to get close to Him just when big things happen—like a death. But not with smaller things—like a job loss or something like that. Like when my kids were little. I remember once when one of my sons cut himself with a knife. He came running to me for help. I gave him first aid, and then I took him to the hospital emergency room. But just as we were leaving, my daughter came with a little sliver in her finger. And I took care of that too. It was just as important to me—because she is my child too.

José: That's interesting. Say more about how that relates to this God you're talking about. How did you get to know all of that?

Art: Well, my parents taught me a lot.

José: Yeah—your parents. My parents don't care about me. In fact, I think they're glad I'm out of the house.

Art: But you don't know that, José. You don't know until you ask them. But in the meantime, you could ask your heavenly Father to make His ways known to you more clearly. To help you understand what He is doing.

José: But how?

Art: Have you ever read the Bible, José?

José: Never.

Art: Ever been to church?

José: I went to a friend's funeral once, but it was weird—holy water and incense and candles and all that stuff.

Art: Church is not the only place where God lives—God is everywhere. But in His Word, the Bible, God can and does speak to us about almost every conceivable subject that we will encounter in life: death, job loss, and alienation from parents. Jesus had personal experience with things like that too. And in the Bible, He shows us how we can get through them.

José: Really? How can I get a Bible?

Art: Well, you could go to a bookstore and buy one. Or you could go to a church. But since you're out of a job, and probably short on money, and you've never been in a church, I might suggest that you could browse the Web. You can get the whole Bible online, you know.

José: Really? But isn't it a really big book?

Art: Yeah. It is. And it sometimes scares me too. But wait. Let me give you our church's Web address. The pastor always has some helpful devotional thoughts online. He's got a new Bible study every week—with the Bible verses printed out right there. You can download it and study it at your convenience.

José: Hey, Art. That's great. Thanks for the tip. I'll check it out. And look, I've got to go, but I'll check with you again next week.

Art: Great. If you have any questions I'll try to help you—or if you like, you could just click on the question box on that Web page. Our pastor is really good about helping. He's a good listener too.

José: So are you, Art. But I wish there was someone close— someone I could just sit down right now and talk to.

Art: Hey, there is. Just check your phone book. Or better yet, I'll give you an address on the Web that you can check for nearby churches. It's not too late. You could call one of them and someone there could help.

José: Gee, thanks, Art.

Art: No problem, José. And let me know if you have any more questions next week. Till then. Bye.

José: Bye, friend. And thanks. By the way, here is something to think about for next week: I know some kids who just got baptized. So what is to prevent me from being baptized too?

Can you imagine the possibilities of sharing your faith online? And networking to other churches all over the country and the world? With computers and the Internet, God has truly placed a powerful tool in our hands. The possibilities are almost without limit, especially in mission fields as technologically advanced as North America.

Note: The Internet is a vehicle whereby people can communicate at random or intentionally with others who are receptive to communicating. This can be in a "chat room" or by other means. People can communicate to and from anywhere in the world for the cost of a local phone call and reasonable monthly service charges from an Internet access provider. There is a definite etiquette for electronic chatting, but general rules of English are often suspended.

FOR DISCUSSION

1. Knowing that God directed us "to the ends of the earth," write down some strategies suggested by Jesus' instructions that you might use to reach others for Christ.
2. If you believe that Jesus Christ is the only name under heaven by which people can be saved (Acts 4:12), how will this affect your speech, actions, and efforts to share Christ with others? Will you go to church more or less often? Will you contribute more or less money to religious and spiritual organizations? Will you volunteer more or less of your time to them?
3. There are probably ways in which you already use technology to enhance your spiritual and religious life. Make a list and share it with someone else to see if you can both expand your lists. (Technology isn't limited to computers!)
4. What limitations exist on using technology to communicate the Gospel?
5. Online with computers and the Internet, there is no age, gender, race, or economic status. Many of the usual obstacles to communication are absent. People are initially anonymous. God made us as individuals. He has called us into a spiritual journey. How might this level of anonymity help in communicating the Gospel? What are the shortcomings, and how can they be overcome?
6. How would you describe your congregation's evangelism and outreach efforts? Do you use Charlie Brown's method, sophisticated target information, or something in-between? How could you improve your methods?
7. If you spend time online in chat rooms or interest groups, what opportunities to witness have you discovered? What were the circumstances?
8. What ideas have you had since you started reading this chapter? Did you write them down? Why not share them with someone else? And may God bless your discussions!

6

OUR RELIGIOUS NEIGHBORS

A QUAINT LITTLE TOWN

It was a beautiful little town with old two-story houses on tree-lined streets. Its picturesque main street was uniformly partitioned with businesses that had been there for years. The names on the storefronts hinted at the European heritage of those who had founded the city 150 years earlier. Many of these shops were still owned and operated by the great-grand-children of the original owners. And clearly visible throughout the town were several church steeples.

Many of these steeples had also been around for years. The tallest was red brick and rose stately, pointing to heaven and claiming preeminence over the rest. The neat white frame church on the west edge of town had a matching white steeple and looked as if it should have been somewhere in New England rather than the Midwest. And another, a more recent addition to the community's religious institutions, wore a shorter, flat-topped bell tower. But it was just as impressive, with ornate carvings all the way to the top.

Most of the town's people belong to one of these three churches, representing major denominations with their roots in Europe. The churches' architecture and traditions had been transplanted to the New World. Even the languages of the founders had been brought along. And in many of the shops along Main Street, and certainly in the barbershop, one could hear the thick accent of German or Norwegian. Until the early part of this century, two of the three churches had maintained worship services in the German language. One of them had to cover up some marvelous artwork during the Second World War because it depicted strong sentiments about the German homeland that had grown unpopular and unpatriotic.

It was a quaint small town. And the people who lived and worked there wanted it to remain that way. Some would secretly admit they feared that more Jewish families would join the two that had come to town decades before. For a long time there had been a healthy ethnic mix among the Germans, Norwegians, and Swedes in the community. But some privately feared an influx of people that would add a mixture of skin color to the cacophony of names that had over the years slowly become familiar. Most kept this secret to themselves, for to express it publicly was neither legal nor Christian. And no one in this quaint small town wanted to commit either offense.

Everyone treasured their neat rows of clean houses and pleasant shops resting along the tree-lined streets. People here accepted change—but slowly and deliberately. Everyone valued the way things had always been and saw no reason for the many changes that seemed so near.

One day everyone was astir. A family came to town looking for a home. Only the mother spoke any English. It was difficult to determine what this new family wanted, but finally one man, a military veteran who had served in the Middle East, was able to understand their needs. They were refugees from Syria, and they had come to settle and open a clothing business in town. Most people were publicly polite. But talk began to circulate as the family searched for a home to rent while they built a new building in which they would live and operate their business.

Not that a good clothing store wouldn't be an asset to this community ... and at this point in conversation, most people's voices began to trail off. They refused to speak what was really on their minds and in their hearts. Many of the people who lived in this quaint little town felt that they accepted change—but it seemed of late that change was coming so fast. And it wasn't as if "outsiders" weren't welcome in town, but, well, they might bring a lot of unwelcome changes. Perhaps there was a place where they could be with "their own kind"!

Think about the changes that have taken place during your short lifetime. It makes no difference if you are 9, 19, 29, or 89; you have seen many changes in the short span of your life.

One change is obvious and nearly universal. Years ago, you had to travel outside the U.S. to see product packaging labels in two languages. Now you notice it in your local store. Many schools in your area offer classes in "English as a second language" and not just for students—but parents and grandparents as well. The ethnic mixture of most metropolitan areas is suggested by the variety of clothing, hairstyles, and cultural expressions, not to mention the surge of new food establishments. These cuisines were once available only at the end of a long flight. Now many are just a short ride from your home.

UNPRECEDENTED CHANGES

The church is also experiencing unprecedented changes. For generations Christians assumed that since our currency boasts the motto "In God we trust," everyone who used dollars as legal tender was a believer—or at least tolerant of believers! But new religions and quasi-religious groups are springing up all over the country. And it is not enough to simply ignore them. Some churches feel threatened by the rise in other religions and cults. Others find this unique situation full of potential for outreach and growth by Christian churches. Orthodox Christianity has to face plurality from a minority. Once people assumed that everyone in their town was Christian. Now these assumptions are challenged daily.

IS FASTEST ALWAYS BEST?

What do you think is the fastest-growing religion in the world today? What about in the United States? What's the best-selling book in the world today? What's the most widely read book in the world today? And what do you think: are "fast" and "most" always best?

The religion of Islam, often incorrectly called Mohammedism, is the fastest-growing religion in the world today. One woman was startled to learn that the headquarters for Islam in her midwestern state were located in a former public school building just blocks from her home. When she knew what to look for, she began to notice people in unusual clothing coming and going at different times each day.

When an Islamic family moved in next door, she got to know the people and found they were friendly. She now knew that unfamiliar clothing had fueled her former hesitancy toward Muslims. She admitted that she hesitated to talk to Islamic women because they sometimes veiled their faces. When she got to know the family next door, she felt more comfortable and began to meet their friends. They engaged in some lively conversations, and although neither the Christian woman nor the Muslims were willing to embrace the religion of the other, all admitted that what they learned by frank and honest conversation helped them understand and appreciate each other. (To learn what Lutherans know about Islam, read *Muslims* by Phillip H. Lochhaas, Concordia Publishing House.)

The Mormon Church is the fastest-growing church in the United States. Founded first by Joseph Smith in New York and later by Brigham Young as he led a remnant of faithful followers to what is today Salt Lake City, this religion has suffered much persecution and misunderstanding. They have a different bible and distinctive marriage practices, and outsiders often perceive them as clannish and difficult to get to know.

It is easy to get false information about any religion by listening to what people say about its adherents. Perhaps the most accurate way to learn about Mormons is to read primary sources—what Mormons say about themselves. We can ask questions of Mormons and their leaders. We can read their literature. But some fear their curiosity will entrap them within the religion, considered a dangerous cult by some and simply a huge business endeavor by others. If you feel the Mormons or any other religious group may use deceptive recruitment tactics, decide how you can guard against entrapment or entering into an argument that you cannot win.

In addition to what the Mormon Church says about itself, learn what others of your faith say about the Mormons. (See *The Latter Day Saints* by Edgar P. Kaiser, Concordia Publishing House, for a Lutheran evaluation.)

Many Mormons revere the Book of Mormon above the Bible. Have you ever looked at a Book of Mormon and compared it to the Bible?

Perhaps if you did, you could discover some common ground upon which to stand as you share your faith in Jesus Christ as the only way to heaven.

If you visit the Mormon world headquarters in Salt Lake City or one of their visitor centers scattered throughout the country, you will learn that they are a well-organized, but not always a well-informed, religious group. Like many religions, individual Mormon believers may not have all the information about what their church believes. (Perhaps this will encourage you to learn more about your own denomination. Ask someone at your church, perhaps your pastor, for information about your religion.)

The Holy Bible is still the best-selling book in the world. But it is not the most widely read book in the world. Can you guess why? Compared to other writings you need for business, hobbies, or pleasure, how often do you read and study the Bible?

GROUND RULES IN TALKING TO YOUR RELIGIOUS NEIGHBORS

Often religious arguments between friends and neighbors end in hard feelings. This is especially serious and potentially divisive when people of differing religions marry. If you want to discuss religion with your neighbors, decide first what ground rules you will follow. Will you use the writings of any other people in your discussions? How do you really know what your religion stands for? What preconceptions do you have about the other religion? What myths do you suspect others have about your religious neighbors? If others hold similar myths about your religion, how do you want them to react to your religion and faith?

Here are some alternatives. How acceptable is each option to you? What others could you add?

1. Tell others you already know what they believe about your religion.
2. Refuse to discuss with others their beliefs about your religion.
3. Inquire what the other person believes about your religion.
4. Together with your pastor or religious leader, involve your neighbor in a discussion about their beliefs.

In discussing grounds rules, agree that arguing probably won't convince anyone. Agree to discuss your feelings. If the discussion has the potential to become divisive, for example for couples who are dating, agree that you will take a time-out and continue the discussion at a later time. Agree to what writings you will use in your discussion. Primary sources, those that are written by people who have personal knowledge of the religion, are usually most reliable. Often people learn about one religion from someone who doesn't have personal experience but only thinks he knows what a particular belief stands for. These are called "secondary" sources.

Some people read and study the Bible but know little more than what others tell them. Consider Jesus' discussion with some religious Jews one day. He challenged them: "You diligently study the Scriptures because you think that by them you possess eternal life. These are the Scriptures that testify about Me, yet you refuse to come to Me to have life" (John 5:39–40).

What is dangerous about seeking "life" in a book or in the rituals of a religion? What would you say to people who think they can get closer to God by vigorous study of the Bible? Jesus told them that "life" came from a relationship with Him.

The following Bible verses and comments may help you to share your faith with others. Do your own research too. Other verses may be helpful in your particular situation.

1. Christian faith involves a relationship with Jesus Christ. "I am the vine; you are the branches. If a man remains in Me and I in him, he will bear much fruit; apart from Me you can do nothing. If anyone does not remain in Me, he is like a branch that is thrown away and withers; such branches are picked up, thrown into the fire and burned" (John 15:5–6). "I am the gate; whoever enters through Me will be saved. He will come in and go out, and find pasture. The thief comes only to steal and kill and destroy; I have come that they may have life, and have it to the full. I am the good shepherd. The good shepherd lays down His life for the sheep" (John 10:9–11).

"My sheep listen to My voice; I know them, and they follow Me. I give them eternal life, and they shall never perish; no one can snatch them out of My hand" (John 10:27–28).

2. The radical nature of the Christian faith involves a change from popular ideas of religion. "You have heard that it was said, 'Love your neighbor and hate your enemy.' But I tell you: Love your enemies and pray for those who persecute you" (Matthew 5:43–44).

"We love because He first loved us. If anyone says, 'I love God,' yet hates his brother, he is a liar. For anyone who does not love his brother, whom he has seen, cannot love God, whom he has not seen. And He has given us this command: Whoever loves God must also love his brother" (1 John 4:19–21).

"If your enemy is hungry, feed him; if he is thirsty, give him something to drink. In doing this, you will heap burning coals on his head. Do not be overcome by evil, but overcome evil with good" (Romans 12:20–21).

3. Christ makes exclusive claim on those who follow Him.

"Salvation is found in no one else, for there is no other name under heaven given to men by which we must be saved" (Acts 4:12).

"Jesus answered, 'I am the way and the truth and the life. No one comes to the Father except through Me' " (John 14:6).

WHAT ABOUT THOSE NEW NEIGHBORS?

As a kid, did you ever struggle with making friends after you moved? What was it like? Were you ever urged or forced to meet some new neighbors? What was that like?

You may have new spiritual neighbors. Maybe you grew up surrounded by churches with familiar names, like Lutheran, Catholic, and Methodist. Now you live in a different place and notice churches with less familiar names like Assembly of God, New Life Church, or Jehovah's Witnesses.

Perhaps you have even encountered expressions of spirituality that don't have a name. You note that coworkers have several strange shapes on their desks. Some people keep "crystals" or pyramids around, believing they are charged with spiritual power. Attributing power to objects like these is a familiar form of idolatry, and it remains foreign to the Christian faith.

Other expressions of spirituality are present in health care, physical fitness, and education. A relatively recent expression of spirituality called the "New Age movement" has broad appeal. This brand of spirituality is profoundly different from traditional Christianity. Informal conversation with "New Agers" may lead you to believe that their religion is similar to yours. They may talk about God moving in your life, doing miracles, and even giving you direction for the future. But upon closer examination you will discover several New Age beliefs that are completely contrary to Holy Scripture. Among these false beliefs are the following:

1. God is not separate from His creation—God and matter are one.
2. People are also one with God—in fact you are a god!
3. All human problems stem from failing to understand that humans are gods.
4. What we need is transformation—to be changed so that we are aware of our oneness with God.
5. That awareness can be changed by techniques that will heighten our awareness of being gods.

These beliefs may anger, worry, or confuse you. What does God say about religious or spiritual expressions like these?

"For the time will come when men will not put up with sound doctrine. Instead, to suit their own desires, they will gather around them a great number of teachers to say what their itching ears want to hear. They will turn their ears away from the truth and turn aside to myths. But you, keep your head in all situations, endure hardship, do the work of an evangelist, discharge all the duties of your ministry" (2 Timothy 4:3–5).

Consider ways that you can arm yourself with "spiritual readiness" to answer challenges to your faith. And then be ready to share the hope that is within you. "But in your hearts set apart Christ as Lord. Always be prepared to give an answer to everyone who asks you to give the reason for the hope that you have. But do this with gentleness and respect" (1 Peter 3:15).

The New Age movement is really a temptation of Satan. He is trying to tear us away from God. When it comes to matters of the Spirit, God warns us always to "test" these spirits to see whether they are of God (1 John 4:1). The easiest test is to determine if your spiritual neighbor believes that Jesus came in the flesh to die on the cross for your sins. If so, then their belief is of God. But if a religious or spiritual belief somehow contradicts your belief in the need for a personal Savior from sin, you must proceed with great caution. The Bible makes this clear through a familiar narrative.

Satan's oldest temptation was to make humans think they were equal with God. He aroused doubt in Adam and Eve concerning

God's goodness in making them perfect. He convinced them that they could indeed be exactly like God—knowing not only good, but also something new—something called evil (Genesis 3:5).

God wasn't pleased when Adam and Eve attempted to put themselves on the same plane with Him. He banished them from the garden and let sin's various miseries punish their sinfulness (Genesis 3:16–24; 11:7–9). The worst consequence of sin is separation from God. (In fact, that's what sin is!) The relationship was broken, and humans from Adam and Eve's time forward could not repair this relationship on their own (Romans 1:17–32).

God did not want humans condemned forever. He promised a Savior to generations of believers, and He delivered that Savior in Jesus Christ. Through His life, death, and resurrection, Jesus restored the relationship between God and people (Romans 12:1–21; Ephesians 2:4–5; Romans 6:3–4).

Christians have a definite afterlife described in the Bible. They know they will rise from the dead, never to die again. Their once-imperfect bodies will be perfect, and they will live with Jesus forever (John 14:6; 1 Corinthians 15:42–44, 54–57; 1 Thessalonians 4:13–18).

You have the greatest message of all times to share with other people: the hope—the certainty—of eternal life because of the shed blood of Jesus Christ. "I write these things to you who believe in the name of the Son of God so that you may know that you have eternal life" (1 John 5:13).

God has given us a wonderful hope by sending Jesus Christ to be with us. May this hope—this certainty—give you a sense of peace forever.

HELLO, NEIGHBOR

For by Him all things were created: things in heaven and on earth, visible and invisible, whether thrones or powers or rulers or authorities; all things were created by Him and for Him. He is before all things, and in Him all things hold together. And He is the head of the body, the church; He is the beginning and the firstborn from among the dead, so that in everything He might have the supremacy. For God was pleased to have all His fullness dwell in Him, and through Him to reconcile to Himself all things, whether things on earth or things in heaven, by making peace through His blood, shed on the cross. (Colossians 1:16–20)

In some ways, other religions are similar to Christianity. They often have a belief in a supreme being, some kind of religious ceremonies, and sacred writings. On the other hand, other religions differ dramatically from Christianity. From the brief portion of Colossians 1 printed above, what other dramatic differences can you think of?

Many natural religions believe that god lives in objects. Christians, however, believe that God is above everything—having created everything. Some other religions try to contact those who have died, but only Christianity claims a Savior who came back from the dead. Blood seems to be important to many religious beliefs. For a Christian, the shed blood of Jesus is all-important!

Perhaps you grew up in a quaint little town or maybe it was a teeming metropolis. Maybe you live in a changeless town or a place that constantly changes. Regardless of where you grew up or where you now live, God has called you to share your faith (Matthew 28:19–20).

We share our hope for a future that is centered in Jesus Christ. As we move into the twenty-first century, there will be many changes in the way we live and express ourselves. We will communicate differently and probably worship at different times and in different places. But we will rest assured that our God will never change.

"Jesus Christ is the same yesterday and today and forever" (Hebrews 13:8).

FOR DISCUSSION

1. List changes that have taken place in your community that demonstrate that variety is the exception rather than the rule in

a. Language and culture
b. Religion
c. Customs
d. Lifestyles and values

2. Assess your comfort level with changes in each of the areas above on a scale of 1 to 10, with 10 being totally comfortable and 1 being very uncomfortable. Explain each of your answers.

3. Which of your religious neighbors follow customs that are significantly different from yours, and what do you know about them?

4. According to the words that follow, who is your neighbor?

   On one occasion an expert in the law stood up to test Jesus. "Teacher," he asked, "what must I do to inherit eternal life?" "What is written in the Law?" He replied. "How do you read it?" He answered: " 'Love the Lord your God with all your heart and with all your soul and with all your strength and with all your mind'; and, 'Love your neighbor as yourself.' " "You have answered correctly," Jesus replied. "Do this and you will live." But he wanted to justify himself, so he asked Jesus, "And who is my neighbor?" In reply Jesus said: "A man was going down from Jerusalem to Jericho ..." (Luke 10:25–30). And so Jesus taught the parable of the Good Samaritan and demonstrated that the unlikely "foreigner" was the one who not only rescued the injured traveler but promised to pay beyond the moment for his care.

   How can you be neighborly, especially to those of a different faith, culture, or language?

5. The word "neighbor" occurs 81 times in the Bible. In Romans 13:9–10, Paul reminds us, "The commandments, 'Do not commit adultery,' 'Do not murder,' 'Do not steal,' 'Do not covet,' and whatever other commandment there may be, are summed up in this one rule: 'Love your neighbor as yourself.' Love does no harm to its neighbor. Therefore love is the fulfillment of the law." How do you love others, especially your neighbor, just like you love yourself?

6. Read the story of Jesus' encounter with a Samaritan woman at Jacob's well in John 4:1–26. What clues can you find to the woman's hesitancy and yet eagerness to interact with Jesus? Why were they culturally ill-matched but spiritually a perfect match?

7. Lepers were required to stand far off and warn others of their dread disease (Luke 17:12). Yet on several occasions, when Jesus encountered lepers, He invited them closer. He talked with them and healed them. What kind of "lepers" might you encounter?

8. Without compromising your faith in Jesus Christ, what can you do to get closer to people of a different culture and faith? How can you listen to what they are saying and not to what you think they are saying? What changes have taken place that increase/decrease your opportunities to become closer to people of a different culture?

9. What beliefs do you hold about other religions that you suspect may not be true? What beliefs do you suspect others hold about your religion that you know aren't true? For example, many Muslims believe that Judas died on the cross instead of Jesus. How could you help a Muslim understand that this is not the truth as taught by the Christian church?

10. Do you think that beliefs such as these are a sign that the end of the world is coming near? How do the "itching ears" (2 Timothy 4:3) of people support beliefs like these? Why do you think people always look for something new?